JEANNE D'ARC

THE MACMILLAN COMPANY
NEW YORK · BOSTON · CHICAGO · DALLAS
ATLANTA · SAN FRANCISCO

MACMILLAN & CO., Limited
LONDON · BOMBAY · CALCUTTA
MELBOURNE

THE MACMILLAN COMPANY
OF CANADA, Limited
TORONTO

SCENE FOR JEANNE D'ARC ACT I (DESIGN BY BARRY FAULKNER)

JEANNE D'ARC

BY

PERCY MACKAYE

AUTHOR OF "THE CANTERBURY PILGRIMS,"
"FENRIS, THE WOLF," ETC.

"Travaillez, travaillez, et Dieu travaillerà."

EIGHTH EDITION
With a New Preface

New York
THE MACMILLAN COMPANY
LONDON: MACMILLAN & CO., LTD.
1935

To

AUGUSTUS SAINT-GAUDENS

IN GRATEFUL REMEMBRANCE

OF RARE INCENTIVES

TO THIS WORK

PREFACE

TO THE EIGHTH EDITION

THE initial production of this play by E. H. Sothern and Julia Marlowe at Philadelphia, October 15, 1906 (followed by a tour in New York, London, and elsewhere) was the first professional production of a play by the writer. Since then, seven editions of the text have been published in separate form before being included in a recent collection of the author's plays. At the present time, with this republication in separate form, a new production of the play is announced to take place at the Greek Theatre, Berkeley, California, in the spring of 1918.

In that interval between the first and latest productions of this play, history has revealed enormous meanings of its theme, kindling the world with the prophetic splendor of Jeanne d'Arc.

Before 1914, the memory of Jeanne moved us as a beautiful legend, a rapture of imagination; to-day, in the great war still raging, her image quickens us with contemporaneous heroism, a rapture of reality.

In that revealing light, no contours of the Maid conceived by imagination in the time before the war can delineate her spiritual stature in reality — a reality immortally fecund, giving millionfold birth to her beauty in the soul of France.

So strangely to-day, after five hundred years, we see Jeanne d'Arc consecrated to a larger leadership than her first call to battle. Born of the people, she has risen anew with her people to champion the deliverance of all peoples. Clear-eyed, unconquerable, she emerges with her country from the mists of feudalism to withstand the last invasion of the feudal despoiler. Under the ruined arches of Rheims, she gathers to her oriflamb not only the children of France but of England, her ancient enemy, and — leagued with two thirds of the risen world — the youth of America. There, anointed by the peoples above all military councils of the Allies, the peasant child Jeanne is our captain.

For America, then, the girl heroine of this play has an intimate meaning poignant at the present time, and even the humblest tribute of an American has its appropriateness to that theme. Indeed it is only by the expression of our deepest sympathies with the idealism of France that we can forge permanently the new fellowship between our peoples based in international hopes and sacrifices.

Such expression must involve not only interchanges political, military, and economic, but others without which these will remain barren of human warmth and beauty — the interchanges of art.

That thought is the reason for this preface.

Even now, while France and America are comrades in battle, we should bethink ourselves of our comradeship in the peace to come: comradeship in the arts of peace, among which the art of the theatre is one supremely powerful.

What consideration are our leaders of thought giving to such expression? What steps of interchange are we planning to take?

Shall our own part be creative and self-reliant, or imitative and filching as in the past? Are our people content merely to patronize Broadway as a centralized department store for importing and distributing indiscriminate foreign wares in drama to commercial branches from coast to coast, or shall we, in national self-respect, at last recognize the theatre's art in all its functional importance, take steps to free it from economic serfdom, and so render it capable of hospitality to foreign artists as its guests, to native artists as its leaders, without corruptive thought of speculation?

An example may serve for suggestion.

During this season in New York, an inspiring precedent has been set on the part of France by Jacques Copeau and his associates in their productions at the Théâtre du Vieux Colombier. There, to the great honor of France and the theatre, Copeau is presenting a repertory which comprises representative works of the classic dramatists — Molière, Corneille, Beaumarchais, La Fontaine, Marivaux, Shakespeare; of the romanticists — Theodore de Banville, Prosper Mérimée, Alfred de Musset; of the moderns — Henri Becque, Tristan Bernard, Paul Claudel, Alphonse Daudet, Dostoievski-Copeau, Roger Martin du Gard, Maeterlinck, Émile Mazaud, Georges de Porto-Riche, Jules Renard, Henri Meilhac, Ludovic Halévy, Auguste Villeroy, Villiers de l'Isle Adam.

Recently, at a meeting in that theatre, the writer was invited to make an address to its members and the public, in the course of which he said, speaking to the Director and the actors:

"At any time you and your work would be significant and welcome. What you have accomplished in France is already a permanent contribution to the art of your country. With high spirit, you have flung your challenge at the feet of Dullness, uttered a glad prayer to your saints of Imagination and Poetry, and struck more than one radical blow for the renascence of Beauty in the theatre.

"But having made this honorable history at home, it is fortunate for us in America that you were not content with that only, and are now come to make international history and to let us share with you in that privilege.

"Lafayette, Rochambeau, Franklin, Washington — to-day these references are much in the mouths of orators and statesmen. Perhaps to some they may grow stale — rhetorical by repetition. Yet such reference to history is timely with truth; nothing to-day is more really alive, nor less merely rhetorical.

"Somewhat over a hundred years ago, here where we now are, the hearts and minds of Americans were on fire for France, and that fire was borne back to France to blaze even more bright and awful in your own history. Our entente then was real; it was fresh and glowing; it was creative. It is not a symbol of rhetoric but of reality — that key of your Bastille which hangs as a trophy, not in Paris, but at Mt. Vernon, America, in the home of Washington.

"Such, then, was our first friendship — ardent, gallant, ennobling. Why did it lapse? Bunglings of politicians, stupidities of commercial rivalries — you immersed in your European rivalries and inner conflicts, we in our vast growth of isolation: so a century passed, during which (let us frankly admit it) we had in each other an interest merely polite, never (since that first glow) passionate in its necessity. In a word, our entente lapsed because we ceased to be fellow workers: we no longer touched hands in a common task.

"Now how changed that all is! For a common task has become the crucible to test our spiritual unity.

"Now our entente leaps to life on a grander — a world — scale. For the issue of our common task is civilization itself — civilization as we hold its philosophy in common, meaning — unsubjugated imagination, liberty to create our destinies according to our own visions, not those of an imposed culture.

"You, then, artists of France, you who come to us with the ancient, the modern, the perennial touchstone of civilization: the art of a great people, you by that token are ambassadors of immense importance, not merely to a few scholars, artists, specialists, or persons precious in culture, but to all our American fighting millions, to every man in the street, to every woman sacrificing for the cause. For your mission represents the heart and soul of that cause — civilization in the highest."

If those words, as I believe, are true, then it is truly worth our while to consider that those high-purposed ambassadors were received neither by our government nor by our theatre; that their coming, almost unheralded, was made possible by a very few enlightened persons of wealth; that no channels whatever exist in our democracy for the appropriate welcoming of such guests bearing priceless gifts of the spirit from people to people. To artists of the theatre in America, this realization should be an arraignment of our theatrical standards; to American citizens — of our standing among the nations.

But whether this realization bears fruit or not, the artists of France and America are already beginning to grope toward mutual service and association in the new age now dawning on the world.

A young poet of France, Pierre de Lanux, has set forth this determined hope, with moving conviction, in a recent volume "Young France and New America" (Macmillan, 1917). A part of his suggested plan implies an interchange in our literatures (including, of course, the drama) through the medium of poets as translators. To the reader of this I commend his ardent pages.

Here I have hoped only to suggest some phases

of the quickening influence in our life which shall spring from our new fellowship with the French Spirit. This play "Jeanne d'Arc" can do no more than attest one writer's long-felt reverence for an immortal child of that Spirit. But the presence of Jeanne d'Arc in the theatre of our time means far more than her name and story as the theme of a play: her anonymous presence in our art born of this war will mean regeneration in our peace.

PERCY MACKAYE.

WASHINGTON, D. C.
22 February, 1918.

CHARACTERS

At Domremy

*JACQUES D'ARC, *father of Jeanne.*

*PIERRE D'ARC, *brother of Jeanne, courting Mengette.*

SEIGNEUR PIERRE DE BOURLEMENT, *proprietor of*
   "*The Ladies' Tree.*"

COLIN, *courting Jeanne.*

GERARD, *home from the English wars, betrothed to Hauviette.*

GERARDIN, *a Burgundian villager, courting Isabellette.*

*PERRIN, *bell-ringer of Domremy.*

*JEANNE D'ARC ("Jeannette"), *the Maid.*

HAUVIETTE, *her girl friend.*

ISABELLETTE, *a peasant girl.*

MENGETTE, *a peasant girl.*

*ST. MICHAEL.

*ST. MARGARET AND ST. CATHERINE.

THE "LADIES OF LORRAINE," *i.e. the Fairies of the*
   Tree.

In France

*CHARLES VII, *King of France.*

*JEAN, DUC D'ALENÇON, *his cousin.*

*SEIGNEUR DE LA TREMOUILLE, *his favorite.*

*REGNAULT DE CHARTRES, *Archbishop of Rheims.*

RÉNÉ DE BOULIGNY, *Receiver-General of France.*

VENDÔME, *the King's Chamberlain.*

*DUNOIS, *French Commander at Orleans.*

*MARSHAL LA HIRE.

*JEAN DE METZ, *of Jeanne's escort to the King.*

*BERTRAND DE POULANGY, *of the same.*

*PASQUEREL, *St. Augustine Friar, Jeanne's Confessor.*

PIGACHON, *Franciscan Friar.*

MASTER SEGUIN, *Dominican of Poitiers.*

BROTHER RICHARD, *a Mendicant Friar.*

*LOUIS DE CONTES, *Jeanne's Page, a boy.*

*PIERRE CAUCHON, *Bishop of Beauvais.*

*NICOLAS LOISELEUR, *of the Inquisition.*

FLAVY, *Governor of Compiegne.*

A TAILOR.

A BOOTMAKER.

*JOHN GRIS, *an English gentleman.*

ADAM GOODSPEED, *an English yeoman.*

AN ENGLISH HERALD.

*CATHERINE DE LA ROCHELLE, ⎫ *Ladies   of   King*
DIANE,   ⎬ *Charles's Court at*
ATHENIE,   ⎭ *Chinon.*

AT ROUEN (Only)

BROTHER MARTIN LADVENU, *a Monk.*

CAPTAIN OF THE ENGLISH GUARD.

THREE ENGLISH GUARDS.

THE VOICE OF THE JUDGE'S CLERK.

SERVANTS, POPULACE, PRIESTS, FRIARS, COURTIERS,
PEASANTS, SOLDIERS.

NOTE.—Characters marked with a star take part in more than one act.

SCENES

ACT I

"The Ladies' Tree," near Domremy; Springtime, 1428.

ACT II

The Castle of King Charles VII, at Chinon; March 8, 1429.

ACT III

A meadow outside the Walls of Orleans; the attack on the Tournelles; May 7, 1429.

ACT IV

Scene I.   *Jeanne's camp before the Walls of Troyes, en route for Rheims; night of July 5, 1429.*

Scene II.   *A street in Rheims, seen from an old wall of the city; Coronation Pageant of King Charles; Sunday, July 17, 1429.*

ACT V

Jeanne's prison at Rouen; May 30, 1431.

ACT I

ACT I

SCENE: "The Ladies' Tree" near Domremy.

Springtime of 1428; a holiday gathering of young folk from the hamlet.

The trunk of the great beech tree, rising toward the back of the scene, left centre, spreads its branches (left) to a group of white birches, in the half concealment of which stands a stone bench. From beneath the branches of the beech (on the right), one looks away to the outskirts of a little French thatched village, more guessed than seen, in the not-far distance. Almost touching the tree-bole (on the left) stands a shrine, with a painted image of the Virgin.

Near this, leaning against the tree, sits a young man (GERARD), dressed — in part — as a soldier, one arm and his breast being bandaged. He watches the boys and girls dancing a country round, in which the latter carry garlands. On the edge of the dance (left) sits a placia group of old women knitting.

The Boys and Girls, taking respective parts in voice and pantomime, sing as they dance.

In green Lorraine, by our Lady's **well,**
  (Rose in flower.)
I picked a rose for a damosel;
  (Weave your garlands!)
I bended low my knee,
   Comme çi!
She makèd courtesy,
   Comme ça!
  Vivo la roso et l'amour!

In green Lorraine, by our Lady's **spring,**
  (Rose in the hour.)
I dropt within the rose a ring,
  (Fetch your garlands!)
And gave it her sweetlỳ;
   Comme çi!
She lookèd long on me,
   Comme ça!
  Vivo la roso et l'amour!

In green Lorraine, by our Lady's **shrine,**
  (Rose in bower.)
Ring and rose she namèd mine;
  (Hang your garlands!)
I threw her kisses three,
   Comme çi!
She tossed them back to me,
   Comme ça!
  Vivo la roso et l'amour!

[*With a finale of tossed kisses and dropt curtsies, the lasses
give their garlands to the lads, who hang them on the*

*trunk of the beech tree, after which all scatter, laughing
and talking, into groups — cracking nuts, love-making,
playing games. In one group (right), playing knucklebone on the grass, is* JEANNE D'ARC, *inconspicuous
amongst the others.*]

ISABELLETTE

[*To Gerardin.*]

Mine hangs too high; they'll have to stand tip-toe
To reach it.

GERARDIN

Who?

ISABELLETTE

The Ladies of Lorraine.

GERARDIN

But who —

ISABELLETTE

Hush, Gerardin; some call them ladies
Some, fairies; but my granny says that they
Long time ago were queens in old Provence
Who fell in love with their own troubadours,
And so were banished by their jealous kings
Far northward to Lorraine; and here, because
They sorrowed with so piteous melody,
Singing the dear songs of their lovers dead,
They won the fairy's hospitality.

GERARDIN

And so these garlands are for them?

ISABELLETTE

Of course!

HAUVIETTE

[*Dancing before Gerard and hugging him.*]
Lon lon, la la, deri dera!

GERARD

[*With a twinge, smiling up at her.*]

My arm!

HAUVIETTE

My poor Gerard! — did she forget his wounds?
Ah, naughty *garçon*, what's he good for now?
Look, Perrin, how they've hacked my fine sweet boy —
The English fiends!

GERARD

Burgundians, they were.

HAUVIETTE

[*To Perrin.*]

'Tis six o' one! They've chopped him up so fine
I'm going to serve him on a silver dish
With lettuce hearts and little parsley leaves —
Ragoût Gerard, avec les petites têtes Anglaises.

[*She laughs merrily.*]

PERRIN

[*Aside.*]

Don't, don't, Hauviette; you know he may not live.

HAUVIETTE
[*Impetuously.*]
Gerard, sweetheart! I love thee!
[*She weeps.*]

GERARD
[*Caressing her.*]
Little swallow!

MENGETTE
[*To Isabellette.*]
Jeannette is on her knees.

ISABELLETTE
Telling her beads?

MENGETTE
No, playing knucklebone there with the boys.

ISABELLETTE
She's brought her knitting with her; think of it!

MENGETTE
Colin will get a good wife.

ISABELLETTE
[*Turning up her nose.*]
Colin? — Pfui!

PIERRE D'ARC
[*Uncovering his face by the tree, shouts.*]
Time!
[*Hunts for others who are playing hide-and-seek with him.*]

TWO GIRLS
[*Dancing together.*]
Asusée !   Asusée !

GERARD
Hauviette —

HAUVIETTE
[*Opening her lunch basket.*]
My fine boy must not talk ; 'tis bad for him.

GERARD
' think —

HAUVIETTE
[*Thrusting it into his mouth.*]
A raisin !

GERARD
But —

HAUVIETTE
An almond !

GERARD
You —

HAUVIETTE
Crack it !

GERARD
I —

HAUVIETTE
Bite ! — a cookie.

GERARD

[*Incoherently.*]

Wish —

HAUVIETTE

A kiss, then!

[*Kisses him on the mouth.*]

PERRIN

[*Cracking nuts with a stone.*]

Heigh, Gerardin! See here — this walnut.

GERARDIN

[*Flirting with Isabellette.*]

Hein?

PERRIN

This here's the Duke of Burgundy — his skull.

[*Smashes the nut loudly. The others laugh and jeer good-naturedly at Gerardin, whose proffered arm Isabellette taking, sticks out her tongue at them.*]

GERARD

[*Laughing back at Perrin.*]

Seigneur the Duke hath brains.

COLIN

[*Thrusting a walnut between his jaws.*]

I crack 'em — so!

GERARD

[*Half rising toward Gerardin.*]

Is he there — ?

HAUVIETTE
[*Standing between them.*]
Hush!

GERARD
Burgundian?

HAUVIETTE
[*Caressing him.*]

Now, now,
If you're not quiet —

GERARD
[*Sinking back.*]
Curse him!

PIERRE D'ARC
[*Creeping stealthily behind Mengette, claps his hand over her
eyes.*]

Name me!

MENGETTE

Pierre!
[*Springing loose.*]
Be still! Here comes the Sieur de Bourlement.
[*General commotion; all who are seated — save Gerard —
get to their feet.*]

GERARDIN
[*Shrugs defiantly and makes a face off right.*]

Who?

ISABELLETTE
[*Horror-struck to Gerardin.*]
My dear, he owns the Ladies' Tree, and half
The land of Domremy.

THE OLD WOMEN
[*Under their breaths.*]

Seigneur de Bourlement!

[*Enter, right,* DE BOURLEMENT. *He strolls in dreamily; in one hand a book; in the other, a walking-stick, which he twirls.*]

DE BOURLEMENT
[*Abstractedly.*]

Good-morrow, dears, good-morrow.

ALL
[*Scatteredly, with bobs and curtsies.*]

Save Seigneur!

DE BOURLEMENT
[*After a pause, during which he reads.*]

Now, now, my pretties, do not stand and stare.
And why are not you dancing? When I saw
You lassies twinkling on the grass, methought
The little marguerites had learned to run.

[*Twirling his cane he drops it. Jeanne springs forward and lifts it.*]

JEANNE

Seigneur — your walking-stick.

DE BOURLEMENT

My wand, Jeannette!
This is the month of May and I am Merlin.

[*Waving his stick.*]

Ask what you will, my lads: 'tis granted you.

COLIN
[*Awkward and loud.*]

I want Jeannette.

[*The others giggle.*]

DE BOURLEMENT

I grant thee, swain — to want her.

[*The others laugh tentatively.*]

Love, Springtime, laughter — *c'est la poesie !*

COLIN

Nay —

DE BOURLEMENT
[*Sniffing the air.*]

Smell, boy ! Smell this day ! and mark what myth
Still lurks i' the nostril : 'tis a charmèd grotto
Where sleeps a nymph, to whom a thousand flowers
Make odorous minstrelsy ; and for her love
The tender lyric of the fleur-de-lys,
The blue-bell's clear *chanson*, the daisy's ballad,
Yea, and the languorous rondel of the rose —
Are all respired. — [*Bowing.*] *Encore la poesie !*

COLIN

I want to wed her.

DE BOURLEMENT
Shepherd, hast thou never
Taken a little walk toward sunset time
Along the fields ? One pauses now and then
To squint the lids, and watch against the west
The cowslip-colour'd light steam from the flocks

To float in haloes 'gainst the quiet clouds;
One sniffs the spearmint by the river's brink,
And waits for dusk-fall, and the twittering
Of swallows overhead, and underneath
The nibbling sound of half-distinguished sheep,
The neatherd's whistle and the colley's bark,
The vesper bell, and with that — voices of angels.

JEANNE
[*Having listened rapt.*]

Amen!

GERARD
[*Who has heard de Bourlement with impatient scorn, tries
to rise.*]
And what of France, Seigneur?
[*Hauviette, frightened, claps her hand over his mouth.*]

DE BOURLEMENT
[*After scrutiny of mild surprise.*]

In France
The dew that fills the lily's cup is song.

GERARD
Song cannot make us men in France, Seigneur,
Nor drive the English bloodhounds from our homes.

HAUVIETTE
Pardon! Oh, sir, he's very ill.

DE BOURLEMENT
Poor boy!
I wish him better. Come, my dears. To-day
Is Sunday of the Wells. Let see which one
Shall win the foot-race to the holy well.

THE YOUNG FOLK

The race!   Outré!

[They crowd about de Bourlement.]

PERRIN

[Seizing Pierre.]

Come to the starting line.

*[Preceded by de Bourlement with his cane, and followed in
the rear by the old knitting-women, exeunt behind the
birches all but Gerard and Hauviette.]*

GERARD
[Gloomily, as Hauviette bends over him.]

Fly with them, bonny swallow ; don't wait here
Beating your slender wings about my eyes.
You cannot blind me, dear ; I see it well
That I am through with life.

HAUVIETTE
                    Tu-whit! to-whoo!
His bonny swallow will peck out those eyes,
If they stare so.

GERARD
Nay, leave!

HAUVIETTE
                    I will not hop
One inch from him.

VOICES
[Shout outside.]
Outré!

HAUVIETTE
[*Jumping up.*]

Ah, hear them now*!*
'Tis the beginning.

GERARD
[*Sinking back.*]
And the ending.

HAUVIETTE
[*Running to the edge of the scene.*]

Oh!
Pierre d'Arc has stuck a rose in Mengette's hair.
She pulled it out, but he has put it back.
Now they've all toed the line; there's five of 'em:
Perrin, Mengette, Pierre d'Arc, Jeannette, and Colin.
Jeannette's between her brother and her sweetheart.

A VOICE
[*Calls outside, with singing intonation.*]
Make ready!

HAUVIETTE
[*Coming back to Gerard.*]
That's the Sieur de Bourlement. — Listen!

THE VOICE
Prepare! — Depart!

HAUVIETTE
[*Rushing back to the edge of scene.*]
Now! Now they're off!

[*Hauviette holds herself tensely with clenched hands.   From outside there come shouts of "Perrin! Pierre! Jeannette!" etc., presently, in the distance, sounding only one name, "Jeannette."*]

Run! Run!

Perrin's ahead. — Ha! — Now! — [*Shouts*] — Jeannette! Jeannette!

Jeannette is winding him. — Faster, Jeannette!

Ah, now they're hid behind the willows. — Peste!

I cannot see.

GERARD

Run after them.

HAUVIETTE

[*Stamping.*]

I won't!

Sacré Maria!   Hark!   Jeannette — she's won!

Thou wretched boy!   Why ever did you fight

Those English ogres?   Now thou art a stump;

Can't race, can't dance, can't play.   O saints! to have

A sweetheart half i' the grave! — Darling Gerard,

Forgive her!   Please forgive her!

GERARD

[*Caressing her, where she snuggles close to him.*]

There, there, there!

[*While Gerard and Hauviette are absorbed in each other thus, boughs of the shrubbery part noiselessly, and Jeanne breaks upon the scene, panting and flushed from running. Not seeing the lovers beneath the beech tree, she seats herself on the stone bench, braids her hair, which has flown loose in the race, takes out her knitting, but lets it fall beside her, fixing her eyes dreamily on the air. Gerard meantime has been playfully humming to Hauviette.*]

My sweetheart's a swallow :
     Her sprite's
     On wing;
Oh, might I follow
     Her flights,
     I'd bring
Back from Heaven the heart of Spring.

[*Hauviette, spying Jeanne, turns Gerard's head and points. Voices in the distance call "Jeannette !"*]

Jeannette ! — What is she doing ?

HAUVIETTE
                     Hiding from 'em ;
Always she's stealing off alone.

         [*Speaking lower.*]
                    They say
She talks with God.

         [*Mischievously.*]
             Let's ask her.

GERARD
                Don't !
HAUVIETTE
[*Bursting suddenly upon Jeanne.*]
                  Hallo !

JEANNE
[*Springs up, startled.*]
Ha ! bon gré Dieu !

       [*Coming to herself.*]
           No one but thee, Hauviette ?

HAUVIETTE

Me and Gerard. — What made you leave the race?

JEANNE
[*Smiling.*]

'Twas finished.

HAUVIETTE

But you won the prize.

JEANNE
[*Shrugging.*]

Just that!

The Jack-o'-ninnies fetched a crown of laurel
To set upon my head.   [*Laughing.*] Ha! but St. John!
I cut away into the underwood
And put 'em off my track.

HAUVIETTE
[*Seeing Isabellette appear through the birches.*]

Look sharp, then.

ISABELLETTE
[*Seeing Jeanne, shouts back.*]

Found!

GERARDIN'S VOICE
[*From without.*]

Where is she?

ISABELLETTE

Here.

[*Enter Gerardin.*]

But hush!

[*With wicked sanctimony.*]

We must not spoil

Mamselle's devotions.

GERARDIN

[*Making a mock bow to Jeanne.*]
                    Pray, Mamselle, forgive
My rude intrusion.

JEANNE

[*Returning a mock curtsy.*]
                    Nay, you're welcome, sir.
God puts a sweet root in the little pig's path,
So we're well met.

GERARDIN

[*Baulked.*]
                    Hein?   Am I root or pig?
[*Enter Colin with a wreath of green leaves.*]

COLIN

Here is thy crown, Jeannette.

ISABELLETTE

                    Pish! not that one!
Run to the window of the kirk, and fetch
Yon little halo made of painted glass —
Sky-blue and gold; she left it by mistake
Last time she prayed there.

HAUVIETTE

                    Run, thou dunderhead!
How shall we get to Heaven without Jeannette?

ISABELLETTE

Yon keys, that dangle at her waist, unlock
St. Peter's wicket.

c

COLIN

Na; I will not go.

HAUVIETTE
[*To Isabellette.*]

I dare you steal 'em.
[*Makes a dash at Jeanne's keys.*]

JEANNE
[*Catching Hauviette's hand powerfully with her left, laughs.*]
If you poke more fun
I'll have your noses all!   One, two, three, four!

[*Snatching at their faces with her right hand, she criss-
crosses the thumb, child-fashion.*]

Now you'll not hold 'em in the air so high.

HAUVIETTE
[*Shaking Jeanne.*]

Wicked Jeannette!   She won't be teased.

ISABELLETTE
[*To Jeanne.*]
But tell!

What made you run away alone?

JEANNE
[*Diffidently.*]
To listen.

ISABELLETTE

Listen!— for what?

GERARDIN

What did you hear?

JEANNE

[*Very quietly.*]

Let's go.

[*As she moves away, the others exchange nods and shrugs.*]

COLIN

Eh! what said I — 'twas them! They be her friends
And keep her company.

JEANNE

[*Turns wonderingly.*]

Who are my friends?

COLIN

The lady wood-folk : I ha' seen 'em with 'ee
Many's the chance at sundown.

ISABELLETTE

Seen them with her?

HAUVIETTE

What — speaking?

COLIN

Like as though.

ISABELLETTE

At sundown?

COLIN

[*Nodding.*]

Darkish.

HAUVIETTE

Where?

COLIN

Here, beside their tree.

JEANNE

　　　　　　　　Thou art wrong, Colin
'Tis well to know that since the good priest read
The gospel of St. John beneath these boughs,
There are no fairies more in Domremy.

ISABELLETTE

O pfui!

HAUVIETTE
[*To Jeanne.*]

You don't believe? — But Colin saw!

JEANNE

Saw moonshine! — I believe my own good eyes
And ears.　*I* never saw nor heard them.

COLIN

　　　　　　　　　　　Eh!
Thy father saith how folk what's spoken to
By fairies knoweth naught of it; but getteth
Gifties most wonderful.

ISABELLETTE

　　　　　　Aha!　That's why
He wants to marry thee, Jeannette.

COLIN
[*Eagerly.*]

　　　　　　　　Aye, that's!
[*Voices shout outside, amidst laughter.*]

GERARDIN

Hark there! Come on! We're missing all the game.

HAUVIETTE

[*Clasping her hands.*]

Ah me! if only I could go!

ISABELLETTE

[*Pulling Hauviette's sleeve as she passes.*]

Come, too!

[*Exit.*]

[*As Gerardin is hastening out, Gerard — with a great effort — lifting his sword in its scabbard, flings it clattering in front of Gerardin, who starts back.*]

GERARD

[*Bitterly.*]

Burgundian!

GERARDIN

You dropt this sword?

GERARD

I flung it

In challenge, sir.

GERARDIN

Bah! I'm no corpse-killer.

[*Exit.*]

HAUVIETTE

[*Exasperated.*]

Stupid Gerard!

JEANNE

[*Bending over Gerard; to Hauviette.*]

Fetch him some water; go.
I'll stay with him.

[*Voices shout outside.*]

HAUVIETTE

[*Calling gayly.*]

I'm coming!

[*Tossing Gerard a kiss.*]

Silly boy!

[*Pulling Colin after her, exit Hauviette. Jeanne, lifting
Gerard's sword reverently, places it by the tree.*]

GERARD

[*Amazed.*]

My sword — your lips have touched it!

JEANNE

God himself
Hath fought with it for France.

GERARD

I fought with it!

JEANNE

And God did clasp His fingers over thine
Along the hilt.   Whoso hath fought for France
Hath fought for Him.

GERARD

Jeannette! you knew, then, why
I flung it there!   You knew?

JEANNE

Full well, my friend.

GERARD

None other knew.

JEANNE

None here besides hath been
Into the battle.

GERARD

Never *you* have been.

JEANNE

Ah me, Gerard, so often have I gone
Amongst the armèd men, methinks I scarce
Have stayed at home.

GERARD

You saw the fighting? When!

JEANNE

Between the shearing and the shearing.

GERARD

Where?

JEANNE

Out there — beyond : in the wide land beyond!
And there were thousands flashing in the sun
Beneath dark walls and mighty battlements,
And all their shining limbs were stiff with steel;
And rank by rank they rattled as they marched,
But each half hid his neighbour with his shield
Like soldiers in the chapel-window glass;

And I rode with them, clad in silver mail
From heel to head, upon a snow-white horse,
And all my oriflammes were painted fair
With lilies and the Rising of our Lord;
For we were marching, midst the roar of bells,
Towards a great cathedral.

GERARD
　　　　　But you dreamed!

JEANNE
[*Changing.*]
Once in the midnight, when I saw them sleeping
After the battle, in the still moonshine
Their linkèd armour lay beside them, sloughed
Like adder skins; and where the living slept,
Their bright breaths rose like candle mist, but on
The dead the dews fell.

GERARD
　　　　　How saw you these sights?

JEANNE
Sometimes I see them very small and bright,
As if they were inlaid in smooth enamel
Like wish-stones in my godfather's thumb-ring.
Sometimes I gaze at them as through clear water,
That moves between us, blurring the deep colours
With skeins of silver when the wind blows.　Ah!
But tell me of the wars which you have seen.
I have great pity for the land of France.
Tell me — for you have fought — what of the wars?

VOICES
[*Outside, amid laughter.*]

Vivo la roso!

GERARD
[*Glooming.*]

Will you not go — play?

JEANNE
[*Smiling.*]

Now think ye they are sighing for me?
[*Adjusting his cloak as a back rest.*]
Move

A little; so is better?

GERARD
It is better.

You asked — what of the wars?

JEANNE
Thou art still in pain

GERARD

Not now; my body's pain is strangely numb, —
What of the wars? Thou knowest the bitter news:
The English are flooded up like the North Sea
Over the fields of France, where all the land
Southward to Orleans drowns with them, and all
The men of France, like moles and field-mice, creep
Under the bloodied furrows.

JEANNE
Orleans stands!

GERARD

Yes; stands like a strong headland in their tide
And will not crumble. Orleans only stands

Between the English army and King Charles.
Yet soon must also Orleans fall, and then —
What hope then for the King?

JEANNE

God fights for him.

GERARD

They say that he is poor and hath few friends,
And daily those desert him, taunting him
That he hath never been crowned.

JEANNE

He shall be crowned.

GERARD

And Burgundy the Duke, the one strong man
Whose right arm should have struck for France, now
    fights
For England and the taste of English gold. —
O God! Jeannette, if thou hadst fought for France,
Now mightest thou feel what 'tis of bitterness
To close my eyes and go down in the dark,
Knowing that even this dust of me must change
Into a little heap of *English* earth.

JEANNE

Gerard! — and you must die?

GERARD

Last night, the doctor
Went from my door to Jacques-the-gravedigger's;
To-day they fetched me here with garlands.

[Rising slowly to her feet, Jeanne holds in her left hand Gerard's sword, and raising her right as one taking a martial oath, speaks with dreamy fervour.]

JEANNE

Listen!

Between Coussy and Vaucouleurs there lives
A girl, that, ere the year is gone, shall save
The land of France, and consecrate King Charles.

GERARD

A girl! — between Coussy and Vaucouleurs?
That's here in Domremy.

JEANNE

Have you not heard
How long ago 'twas spoken, "Out of Lorraine,
Beside the Ladies' Tree, shall come a maid —
Saviour of France"?

GERARD

This is the Ladies' Tree!

JEANNE

And truly was it spoken. — I am the Maid.

GERARD

Jeannette!

JEANNE

It hath been told me.

GERARD

Who hath told?

JEANNE

The Lord hath sent His angel, even St. Michael,
To me, Jeannette.

GERARD

Thou hast beheld him?

JEANNE

Yes.

GERARD

And heard him speak?

JEANNE

Often.

GERARD

When was this?

JEANNE

First

Four years ago. 'Twas in my father's garden;
I was then but thirteen; I heard his voice.
It was mid-day, in summer; I was frightened.
I had not fasted on the day before.
A little to my right, towards the church,
I heard it; on one side there shone a light.

GERARD

What! — in the noon time?

JEANNE

Yes; a burning light.
It dazzled me; and then I saw his face.

GERARD

Alone?

JEANNE

It was surrounded all with angels,
That glittered like the little poplar leaves
Behind our barn.

GERARD

You saw them bodily?

JEANNE

I saw them with these eyes as clearly as
I see you there.   Just then the mass bell rung,
And then St. Michael spoke.

GERARD

Mind you what words?

JEANNE

He said: " Jeanne d'Arc, thy Lord hath chosen thee
To save the land of France.   When I am gone,
St. Catherine will come and Margaret,
His saints, to counsel thee."

GERARD

More did he say?

JEANNE

"Be good and wait," he said; and then once more
"Be a good girl, Jeannette," he said; and so
He and his angels went away, and I
Wept, for I would have liked to go with them.

GERARD

St. Catherine and Margaret — they came?

JEANNE

Often they come.

GERARD

You have seen them also?

JEANNE

Yes;

But oftenest I hear them speak; I call them
" My Voices," and I hear them when the bells
Are ringing — more at Matins and at Vespers
Than other hours.   At first they counselled me
But to be good, and to prepare myself
Against St. Michael's coming.   But of late
They have forewarned me I must go to raise
The siege of Orleans and have crowned the Dauphin.

GERARD

[*Ardently.*]

For what, then, dost thou wait, Jeannette?

JEANNE

St. Michael,

His coming.

GERARD

Ah! and will he come again
Before — I go?

JEANNE

My Voices warn me oft
That he at any moment may appear
And bid me go unto Chinon, the Castle
Of Charles the Dauphin, and make known to him
My mission from cur Lord.

GERARD

He will believe!
Jeannette, he will believe, as I! — O France,

Out of Lorraine hath come the Lord His maid
To succour thee in thy death peril!

JACQUES D'ARC
[*His voice heard outside — left.*]
Colin!
JEANNE

My father! Tell him not. I have not leave
To tell yet what I know. You I have told,
For you must soon go hence before my saints,
And will explain my trespass.

GERARD

I will tell them
How you revealed their secret to one dead
And made him happy.

JEANNE
[*Watching her father approach outside.*]
He would grieve, besides,
And rage, and would not let me leave him.
[*Enter Jacques d'Arc and Colin.*]
Hush!
JACQUES
[*To Colin.*]
Round up the sheep with me.

COLIN
[*Follows slowly.*]
Where keepst thy dog?

JACQUES
Suckleth her whelps at home. Hark yonder! Yon's

The bell-wether, hath jumped the pound. — Good e'en,
Jeannette. Aye, knitting, hein ?

JEANNE

God give good e'en.

JACQUES

What for not making holiday ? 'Tis Sabbath ;
Seigneur himself walks yon with the young folk ;
And Colin there clapt to 't with another sweetheart, —
Ah, Colin ?

COLIN

[*Jerking his thumb at Jeanne and Gerard.*]

She would browse with the lame sheep.

JACQUES

[*To Jeanne.*]

What for with *him?*

GERARD

She asked me of the wars.

JACQUES

The wars? Hark here, lass. Drop that gabble ;
drop 't,
I warn thee, down the nighest well and bury 't.
No maid o' mine shall gossip o' the wars
With any man. — And hast forgot my dream,
Jeannette ?

JEANNE

No.

JACQUES

Ofttime dreams be perilous.
I saw thee in my dream fighting for France,
And thou wert bleeding at the breast. May God

Forgi'e 't me!— Ere thou went to war, Jeannette,
I'd have thy brothers drown thee.
> [*Turns away, speaking to Colin.*]

> Where's thy staff?

COLIN

Over against the sheep-pound.
> [*There run in Hauviette, Mengette, Pierre, Ferrin, and
> Others.*]

PERRIN

> Fetch Gerard!

JACQUES
> [*To Colin.*]

Come!— Wait for me, Jeannette; we'll home with 'ee.
> [*Exeunt Jacques and Colin, right.*]

HAUVIETTE

Gerard, Gerard, three kisses!   Then up, up!

GERARD

Where is the swallow flying!

HAUVIETTE

> With the flock

Of course.

MENGETTE

> You're coming with us?

PIERRE

> To be cured.

HAUVIETTE

We're going to the well of thorns; Seigneur
Is waiting for us.   'Tis a sacred well,

D

And filled with holy water to the brim;
And when you drink of it, you will be cured.

PIERRE

Make him a chair.

SEVERAL OTHERS
A chair!

[*Pierre and another lad by interlacing their hands form a seat
into which Gerard is raised.*]

PERRIN

Now up with him!

[*Lifted by the two lads, Gerard is carried off, surrounded by
the others shouting.*]

GERARD
[*From his chair of hands.*]

Good-by, Jeannette; I'm going to be cured.

JEANNE
[*Waves to him.*]

Adieu, Gerard!

THE OTHERS
[*Going out.*]
Outré! Gerard! Gerard!

JEANNE
[*To Perrin, as he is leaving with the others.*]

Perrin!

[*Perrin pauses and looks at Jeanne, who shakes her finger
at him with a grave smile. He drops his eyes, con-
fused.*]

PERRIN

But 'tisn't late.

JEANNE

The sky's all pink
And gold behind the bell-tower.
[*Turning him toward the shrine.*]

Naughty Perrin !
What will Our Lady say, who leaneth there
And listeneth for her Vesper bell, and heareth
Perrin at play.

PERRIN

I cannot ring just yet.
The others —

JEANNE

[*Thrusting her knitting into his hands.*]

Here's a mitten ; 'tis of wool.
I'll knit thee its fellow before Michaelmas
If thou wilt run fast to the kirk, and ring
The bell.

PERRIN

Our Lady shall not scold, then. — Mind,
Thou'lt knit me t'other mitten ?

JEANNE

I have promised.
[*Perrin runs off toward Domremy. Jeanne, going slowly to
the Ladies' Tree, leans against the trunk, and stands
looking westward toward the town. As she does so,
there rises — faint but close by, through the falling twilight — a music of sweet voices, singing to the old French
ballad-melody these words, softly distinguishable.*]

THE TWILIGHT VOICES

Derrièr' chez mon père,
    (Vole, vole, mon cœur vole !)
Derrièr' chez mon père
    Y'a un pommier doux :
        Tout doux — et iou !
        Tout doux — et iou !
    Y'a un pommier doux.

Trois belles princesses
    (Vole, vole, mon cœur, vole !)
Trois belles princesses
    Sont assis dessous :
        Tout doux — et iou !
        Tout doux — et iou !
    Sont assis dessous.

Ça dit la première, vole, etc.
    Je crois qu'il fait jour.

Ça dit la seconde — etc.
    J'entends le tambour.

[*Jeanne, pensive, does not hear the melody, nor observe how near her, from amid the obscurity of the birch trees, there emerge the shadowy forms of the* LADIES OF LORRAINE. *Each of these peers forth from her own bush or birch or flowering shrub, to which her garb — with its long green veil and flowing forest gown — approximates in tone and design.*[1] *Each wears a crown and has an air at once queenly and sylvan.*]

[1] Thus the veil of the Lady of the Flowering Thorn is embroidered all with thorn blossoms; the gown of the Lady of the Aspen twinkles and shivers with little leaves.

THE LADIES OF LORRAINE
[*Continuing.*]

Ça dit la troisième — etc.
C'est mon ami doux.

Il va-t-a la guerre — etc.
Combattre pour nous.

[*Ceasing, none of the Ladies entirely dissociates herself
from her bush or tree, but peering forward, all together,
they lift from their brows, and hold aloft with their right
hands, their crowns and fillets and therewith lay a spell
upon Jeanne, who — outwardly oblivious of their presence — yet is felt to soliloquize under their influence, not
beginning to speak until they appear, and ceasing simultaneous with their abrupt departure.*]

JEANNE
[*By the Ladies' Tree.*]

How happily doth all the world go home!
The bee hath left the shutting marguerite
To dust his wings at Pierrot's garden-door
And hum all night to drowsy chanticleer;
The rooks are whirling to the nested eaves. —
Thou little darling town of Domremy,
Good night! Thou winkest with thy lids of vines,
And layest down within the golden stream
Thy yellow thatches and thy poplars pale;
And thou, too, art upgathered in home-fields;
But thy Jeannette must pass away from thee.
For He who once disdainèd not to stay
His wandering star o'er tiny Bethlehem
Hath, in His love of France, sent unto thee

His shining messengers to fetch thy Maid.
O little town, hush still thy breath and hark!
Amid thy narrow streets are angels arming,
And o'er thy steeping-stones immortal feet
Are bearing light the undying fleur-de-lis;
And from thy roofs clear horns-of-Paradise
Are blowing wide unto the zenith : Hearken!—
Who shall withstand the Lord of Hosts, or who
Defy His power?   The horses of the Lord
Are neighing, terrible; His chariots
Of thunder crash in darkness, and the voice
Calleth of His Archangel from the battle :
"Vive la France!   Victoire!   La France sauvée!"

JACQUES D'ARC
[*Outside.*]

Along!   Along!

[*The Ladies vanish in the foliage. Jeanne stands as in a
        trance. Enter right Jacques, grasping by the wrist
        Colin, who holds back, quaking.*]

Where be they?   Show me where?

COLIN

Na, na; I'll not come nigh her.   They be gone
Inside.

JACQUES

Inside o' what?

COLIN

The bark and roots:
I saw them yonder lifting o' their veils.

JACQUES

Where?

[*Colin points.*]

Those be birches.

COLIN

Ladies were they then,
And peered and peeped at her.

JACQUES

At who?

COLIN

Jeannette;
I'll not come nigh her.

JACQUES

[*Visibly affected, yet will not show it to Colin.*]

Pfah! Thou hast such visions
As Pertelote, our hen: spyeth the moon,
And cackleth she hath laid our Lord an egg. —
Jeannette o' mine, come hither.

JEANNE

[*Breaking from her revery, goes impetuously to his arms.*]

Papa Jacques!

JACQUES

[*Embracing her tenderly, looks toward the birches.*]

Th' art a good lass, Jeannette. I spake thee harsh
Awhile since.

JEANNE

Will I scold thee for it now?

JACQUES

A good lass was thou always; — but some stubborn.

JEANNE

Like Papa Jacques?

[*Kisses him.*]

JACQUES

>   Aye, Jacques d'Arc hath a will.
Th' art come short-cut thereby !   But hark'ee, girl!
Shut mouth catches no flies. — I'll have thee speak
No more o' the wars. — What say ?   I'll have thee be
Like other village maid-folk — light o' heart,
Merry to love. — Eh, not ? — I'll have thee wed,
And keep thy goodman's sheep-farm next to mine.
Come now : What say to Colin ?

JEANNE

>   'Tis a good lad.

JACQUES

St. John !   'Tis a good answer.   Once again !
What say to speak him troth now — man and maid ?

JEANNE

I may not speak my troth to any man.

JACQUES

May not!   *May* not!   Who's thy new master, sith
Thy father died ?   Who hath forbade thee speak ?
Well, well; let be !   Thou needst not *speak* thy troth.
Look : yonder, Colin holds his sheep-staff out
Toward thee ; take it, lass, and nothing spoke —
In token of thy trothal.

[*Jeanne, gazing apparently at Colin, clasps suddenly her
>   hands in awe, and makes a humble reverence.*]

JEANNE

>   Monseigneur !

Thy maid is ready.

JACQUES
[*Who has turned away.*]
          Take 't and come along.

JEANNE
[*To Jacques.*]
What is that which you see held forth to me?

JACQUES
Seest well thyself 'tis Colin's staff.   What for
Art staring?

JEANNE
          'Tis exceeding beautiful
In glory and in power; its handle gleams
Bright as the cross of jewels at the mass,
And oh, its sheath is like an altar-candle.

[*In the distance a bell begins to ring slowly. Jacques bows
his head. Colin, awed by Jeanne's words and expression, thrusts the staff upright in the earth and steps
back a pace from it, superstitiously.*]

JACQUES
[*Crossing himself.*]
The Vespers.

JEANNE
[*Sinking to her knees.*]
          Monseigneur!

[*At this moment in the air beside Colin appears the glorified
form of* ST. MICHAEL. *Shepherd and Archangel stand
contrasted, yet alike in posture, looking toward Jeanne.*]

JACQUES
                    Up, lass!   What aileth?
Wilt take the sheep-crook?

JEANNE

Wilt thou have me take
What in the turf stands yonder?

JACQUES

In God's name!

JEANNE

In God's name, then, I take it.

[*Reaching out, she pauses and draws back — her face lifted
to St. Michael's — as, in the cadence of the bell, he
speaks.*]

ST. MICHAEL

[*Slowly extending his hand.*]

Jeanne the Maid,
Behold the staff I bring thee is my sword.

[*Lightly laying his hand upon the staff, instantaneously his
touch transforms it to a perpendicular sword, its point
piercing the turf, its cross-formed handle and its sheath
glowing with variegated fire.*]

Take it in vow of thy virginity,
And to perform the bidding of thy Lord —
That thou, in armour girded as a man
Shalt go to raise at Orleans the great siege,
And after, crown the Dauphin, Charles of France,
Anointed King at Rheims.

COLIN

[*Pointing.*]

The crook, Jeannette!
Take it in troth.

ST. MICHAEL

[*Pointing.*]

Take it in troth, Jeanne d'Arc.

JEANNE

In God His name, I take it as from Him
To whom my vow is given.

*[Extending her hand, Jeanne touches the sword; then bows
her head as St. Michael disappears.]*

JACQUES

So ; she hath touched
Thy staff in trothal, lad.   Now home with ye
Together.

COLIN

Come, Jeannette.

JEANNE

First, I will pray.

JACQUES
[Aside to Colin.]
The Vespers ! — Come along. — She'll follow us.

COLIN
[Going out, sings.]
Sith for Charity
My love her troth me gave,
My troth hath she
I *her* have.

*[Exit Colin.   Jacques, looking back at Jeanne, crosses him-
self, muttering, and exit.   Twilight deepens.   Blending
with the tones of the chapel bell are heard two Voices.]*

THE FIRST VOICE
Jeanne d'Arc!

JEANNE
[Calling.]
St. Margaret !

THE SECOND VOICE

Jeanne la Pucelle '

JEANNE

St. Catherine!

THE TWO VOICES

Daughter of God, go forth!

[*Jeanne, on the turf, kneels before the cross of the shining sword. Vespers continue to ring.*]

ACT II

ACT II

An audience-hall, sparsely furnished with an indigent mag-
nificence.

The chief entrance at back is in the centre. On the right of
this an ornate clock, with chimes. On the left, high in
the wall, a stained-glass window depicts the Emperor
Charlemagne, with the shield of France, holding a
crown. Against the left wall, a throne-chair with
canopy; in the right wall, a fireplace with chimney-seat.
At the oblique angle of the right and back walls, a stair-
way descends from a colonnade, partly visible without.

The scene, opening, discovers KING CHARLES *seated on an*
arm of the throne-chair, with one foot on the seat, the
other crossed over his knee. Round his neck, behind,
is hung a placard, lettered in red and gold :

LE ROI

DAGOBERT

C'EST MOI

He is surrounded by LADIES *of the Court, who are merrily*
shouting a song, whilst they watch the royal TAILOR,
who bends assiduously over the King's crossed leg, ply-
ing his thread and needle. Beside him stands his spool-
and-shears basket.

Apart from these, at a table near the fire, are seated LA
TREMOUILLE *and* DE CHARTRES. *The former is busily*
engaged in looking over a pile of parchments. From
time to time he is approached with great reverence by
servants and courtiers.

THE LADIES
[*Sing to the old ballad-tune.*]

'Twas good King Dagobert
His breeches wrong-side-out did wear.
Quoth his Master of Stitches:
"Your Majesty's breeches,
To put it mild strongly,
Are put on well wrongly."
"Eh bien!" the King he cried,
"Just wait and I'll turn 'em right side."

LA TREMOUILLE
[*To* VENDÔME, *the Chamberlain.*]

This seal to the Receiver-General;
These parchments to the Treasurer of War.

THE LADIES

God save King Dagobert!

THE TAILOR
                    Good Majesty
Doth wear the seam outside.

CHARLES
                    Why not, old Stitches?
I'll set the fashion so; I am chafed too long
With wearing o' the seamy-side *within.*

CATHERINE
[*Aside to* DIANE.]

Still munching the old cud of melancholy —
His mother.

CATHERINE

DIANE

Why his mother?

CATHERINE

Shh! They say

She called him —

DIANE

Hein?

CATHERINE

They spell it with a "b."

ATHENIE

Imperial Dagobert, permit thy slave
To be thy needle-woman.

CATHERINE

Nay, let me;

My silk is threaded.

DIANE

'Twere a thousand pities
To wholly sheathe so glorious a sword!

[*Touching the King's leg.*]

Is it of gold?

CHARLES

Ah, lady, would it were,
And I would lend it out at usury
To line your purse withal. — Alas, madame,
'Tis a poor limb charr'd with celestial fire.

[*Waves her back.*]

CATHERINE

Ladies, we may not look. We must content
Our souls with incense of the burning thigh.

DE CHARTRES

[*To La Tremouille, amid the Ladies' laughter.*]

Is it possible ?

LA TREMOUILLE

They are his only pair ;
The rest he pawned this morning.   These being torn,
He calls the tailor and commands the ladies
To acclaim him as King Dagobert.

DE CHARTRES

What for ?

LA TREMOUILLE

For novelty.   One day he'll hang himself
For novelty.

THE TAILOR

Your Majesty is mended.

CHARLES

Approach, mesdames, and view the royal patch.

ATHENIE

But where ?

CATHERINE

I cannot see it.

CHARLES

Even so !

Your patch is virtue's own epitome,
The smooth'd-up leak in honour's water-mark,
The small fig-leaf that shadows Paradise,
The tiny seal of time and turpitude.
Which for to prove, sweet dames, bethink you how
The great Achilles — he who fought and sulked

Outside the walls of Troy — was once a babe,
(Babes will occur, mesdames!) and had a mother
(The best of us have mothers, though not all
Be goddesses). His mother was called Thetis,
And when she dipped him in the immortal wave,
She held him by the heel — thus — thumb and finger,
That ever afterward upon the heel
He wore a patch — a little viewless patch,
Whereby he came to dust. The moral's plain:
A little patch is greater than a god,
And therefore this your prince, poor Dagobert,
Doth kiss his hands to you and abdicate
In lieu of one more royal lord — King Patch.
Acclaim him!

[*Stepping down, Charles mounts the Tailor upon the throne,
on the seat of which he stands, in alarmed confusion.*]

THE TAILOR

Majesty! — Sweet ladies!

THE LADIES

Hail!

CHARLES

Behold the man who mendeth Alexander,
And ravelleth up the rended Cæsar's wounds:
Lo! moth corrupteth us, and mildew stains,
Diana frays her moon-white taffeta,
Yea, Phœbus sullieth his golden hose,
Fate makes or mars us, but King Patch doth mend!

BOULIGNY

[*Having just entered, claps his palm.*]

Par excellence, a Cicero!

E

CHARLES
[*Bowing.*]
Your servant,
Bouligny!—now to crown him, ladies.

THE LADIES
Crown him!

[*Catherine snatches up the work-basket and, inverting, lifts it — dangling with spools, bobbins, and shears — toward the Tailor.*]

THE TAILOR
Dames! Gentle dames!

CATHERINE
[*Thrusting the basket over his head.*]
A crown!

DIANE
[*Forcing a yardstick into his hand.*]
A sceptre!

THE TAILOR
[*From within the basket.*]
Virgin!

ALL
Long live King Patch!

[*The Tailor, extricating himself, giggling and grinning a scared smile, bobs and kisses his palm to Charles and the Ladies, who shout with laughter.*]

THE TAILOR
Pardon and compliments!
Pardon, mesdames, seigneurs, and compliments!

[*At the height of this royal mockery, there enters from the colonnade,* D'ALENÇON — *a quiet, contrasting figure. He
is scribbling on a parchment and pauses. Glancing
from the throne-chair scene, he turns to where La Tremouille and De Chartres are talking together apart,
and silently approaches them.*]

LA TREMOUILLE
[*Pointing at the Tailor.*]
Behold the King of France enthroned.

DE CHARTRES
You mean
That we must strive to keep him thus.

LA TREMOUILLE
I mean
That he who holds a mortgage on a king
May keep the sceptre for security
During the debt's outstanding.

DE CHARTRES
How the sceptre?

LA TREMOUILLE
The power, De Chartres; like yonder Knave of
Spools
Charles wields the royal yardstick, but the King
Of France — the man that *reigns* — c'est moi!

DE CHARTRES
And I?

LA TREMOUILLE
[*Graciously.*]
My privy council.

[*Suddenly; over his shoulder observing D'Alençon.*]
Ah, D'Alençon ! —

Poeticizing ?

D'ALENÇON
Yes ; I am composing
A rondel on the weather, called " *It rains.*"

[*De Chartres and La Tremouille glance at each other quizzi-
cally. With a studious look D'Alençon turns away, and
takes from the fireplace a book.*]

THE COURT LADIES
A speech ! A coronation speech !

THE TAILOR
Mesdames,
Seigneurs, and compliments ! If Majesty
Would pay to me my wage, and let me go.

CHARLES
Thy wage, *par dieu !* O heart of emery !
Sharpen your needles in him, ladies. Wage !
Wage for a patch !

THE TAILOR
Nay, Majesty, a year —
One year, last Candlemas, 'tis overdue.

CHARLES
Hark to the bobbin buzz ! What, take thy wages !
Wilt bear 'em on thy back ? A twelvemonth, here !
One month — two — three — four !

[*Snatching from him the yardstick, Charles thwacks the
Tailor down from the throne, whence he runs, pursued
by the Ladies, who prick his sides with their needles.*]

THE TAILOR
[*Running off.*]

Charity, mesdames!
[*Exit.*]

CHARLES
[*Pauses, laughing, and greets D'Alençon, who, over his book, has been looking keenly on.*]
What think you of our royal sport, D'Alençon?

D'ALENÇON
No king, sire, could more quaintly lose his kingdom.
[*Charles, ceasing his laughter with a conscious look, vaguely ashamed, hesitates, then follows D'Alençon, who has turned away, and — walking aside with him — grows strangely serious.*]

LA TREMOUILLE
[*To De Chartres.*]
Behold my Rome and Rubicon.

DE CHARTRES
What — yonder?
LA TREMOUILLE
That man is in my way; he must be crossed
Before the King is mine.

DE CHARTRES
That bookworm duke!

LA TREMOUILLE
His influence grows.

DE CHARTRES
Nay, hardly with the King!

LA TREMOUILLE

De Chartres, you know not Charles; he's like a tree-
    frog
That takes the colour of the bark it clings to.
Watch how demure he holds the young duke's sleeve
And alters to the dim scholastic hue
Of vellum and antique philosophy ;
As quickly would he turn blood-colour, if
The duke should flush with feeling.

DE CHARTRES

                    Feeling ! Flush ?
Why, 'tis a rhyming clerk ! — a duke of parchment !
The mere illumination of a man
Stuck in life's margin to adorn the text.
He *feels* for naught this side the Fall of Troy.

LA TREMOUILLE

You have forgot " It rains " ?

DE CHARTRES

                    A foolish pun !

LA TREMOUILLE

About *myself :* that theme, at least, is new
Since Troy fell.   No ; I do not trust him. — You
Were best to interrupt their tête-à-tête.

VENDÔME

[*At the door, announces to Charles.*]
His Majesty's bootmaker !

CHARLES

                    Show him here.

DE CHARTRES

[*As Charles turns momentarily toward Vendôme, touches D'Alençon's volume and speaks to him.*]

Who wrote the book ?

D'ALENÇON

                    Pierre Lombard, pupil once
Of Abelard, who sang to Heloise.

DE CHARTRES
[*Frowning suspicion.*]

Is it godly ?

D'ALENÇON

                    That your reverence may judge :
The writer plucks a hair out of his head,
Splits it in two, and names the one half Faith
The other, Heresy.   The first he dyes
Pure gold, the other pitch-black, and both he nails
As index-fingers on the Church's apse,
And points one hair toward Heaven, the other —
        elsewhere.

DE CHARTRES
I do not comprehend.

D'ALENÇON

[*Closing the book with a dry smile.*]

                    Neither do I !

[*Exit D'Alençon, right.*]

LA TREMOUILLE

[*To De Chartres, who returns pensively to him.*]
What think you now ?

DE CHARTRES
I think *he* thinks too much.

[*Enter the* Bootmaker, *a big raw fellow, in leather.
He takes a pair of boots from his apron.*]

BOOTMAKER
Complete, sire.

CHARLES
Let me see them.
[*The Bootmaker hands him one.*]
Catherine,
What say you to the cut?

CATHERINE
Perfection, Charles!
Your Majesty shall walk like Puss-in-Boots
When he proclaimed the Marquis of Carabbas.

CHARLES
[*With sudden ennui, comparing the boot with his lower leg.*]
Perchance 'twill serve to hide Achilles' heel?
[*To the Bootmaker.*]
Show me the mate.

BOOTMAKER
Six livres, twenty sous.

CHARLES
The mate, I said.

BOOTMAKER
[*Stolidly, thrusting the mate under his arm.*]
Six livres, twenty sous.

CHARLES
Ah? Charge it on account. I'll take the pair.

BOOTMAKER
[*Inflexible.*]

A bird in the hand makes supper in the pot.

CHARLES

God's death! Am I the King? Set down the boot
And go!

BOOTMAKER
[*Backing to the door, stands sullenly, swinging the one boot
by its straps.*]

Six livres, twenty sous.

CHARLES
[*Hurling the other boot after him.*]

Go dun

The devil for it!

BOOTMAKER
[*Picking up the boot, eyes it over, spits on his apron, and
with that rubs the toe of the boot carefully.*]

Five and twenty sous!

[*Exit slowly, a boot in each hand. Charles, having
watched him go, turns in a pet of frenzy and, flinging
down upon the throne footstool, speaks hoarsely to himself, weeping.*]

CHARLES

Am I the King? God, God! *Am* I the King?

DE CHARTRES
[*Amused, to La Tremouille.*]

Have you no smiles for this?

LA TREMOUILLE
[*Yawning.*]

'Tis too familiar.

CATHERINE

[*Approaching La Tremouille, obsequiously.*]

The little King of Chinon hath caught the sulks,
Sieur La Tremouille.

LA TREMOUILLE

I'm busy.

CATHERINE

Pardon —

[*With an ingratiatory lifting of the brows and a low
reverence.*]

— Sire ?

[*La Tremouille smiles slightly and looks down again at
his papers. As De Chartres, however, leaves the table
to speak with Bouligny, La Tremouille calls Catherine
with his eyes, and speaks to her intimately, watching
with her the King and smiling.*]

ATHENIE

[*To* LA HIRE, *who enters.*]

Marshal, hast heard what ails the King's game-cocks ?

LA HIRE

No, dame.

ATHENIE

'Tis said that they have shed their spurs,
And strut amongst the hens i' the castle-yard
　　　[*Flaps her sleeves like a cock's wings.*]

Crying : " King Noodle-Nothing-Do !　*Chez nous !* "

[*La Hire turns away with a grimace.*]

DIANE

[To a Lady.]

No wonder the King's figure is god-like.
They say his lady mother had a steward
Shaped like Apollo.

CHARLES

[From the footstool.]

               Ladies, I have the ear-ache.

DIANE

Beseech you, sire, what may we do to soothe it?

CHARLES

Bring here those honey-flasks of calumny
And pour them in my ears.   Perchance 'twill stop
This piping noise within.

ATHENIE

               What piping noise,
Your Majesty?

CHARLES

        A lute within my head:
A slender lute carven with fleur-de-lis,
And at the tip a crown of fleur-de-lis,
And on the stops a lady's fingers lying,
And on the mouth-piece are a lady's lips,
And when they breathe, there opes a tiny rift
Within the fibre, and the hollow thing
Pipes a shrill hellish whistle —

[Leaping up.]

               A mere rift,
A little, little rent! —

LA TREMOUILLE
Nine thousand francs!

CHARLES

What's that?

LA TREMOUILLE
[*With a side smile at Catherine.*]
The "little rent" you owe me, Charles.
A trifle, as you say, and soon patched up.

CHARLES

My George! Thou hast a heart of gold!— But you
Must reimburse yourself o' the treasury.
Bouligny!

BOULIGNY
Sire!

CHARLES
How much in the general fund?

BOULIGNY

Eleven francs, five sous, your Majesty.

CHARLES

Saint dieu! no more than that?

BOULIGNY
Sieur La Tremouille
Hath authorized to-day another loan
From his estates.

CHARLES
[*Embracing La Tremouille.*]
My dear, thou art mine angel!

LA TREMOUILLE

Tut, Charlie! Go and play.

CHARLES
Nay, by my honour,
But you shall reap your master's gratitude.
When we have raised our arm imperial
And flogged with steel these spindling English —

[*The room bursts into a titter; Charles pauses disconcerted.
La Tremouille, badly concealing a smile, raises an
admonishing forefinger to the Ladies, who burst into
louder laughter. Charles, covering his face, turns
precipitately and is rushing from the room when, in
the doorway (back) he encounters D'Alençon, entering.
The latter has evidently just been concerned with the
frayed edges of his scroll of parchment, but now — taking in the situation at a glance — he bows to the King
with simple reverence.*]

D'ALENÇON
Sire,
You are generous to cover my confusion.
Yet if these gentles choose to laugh at me —

CHARLES
[*Bewildered.*]
At *you !*

D'ALENÇON
Why, they are right. You spoke of war,
Of frays where brave men break their limbs and
lances,
When lo ! — I enter, mending of a parchment.
Should not they laugh ? 'Tis such as I, my King,
Such dog-eared captains skulking in their books,
Such Frenchmen, idling in satiric ease
While France lies struck and bleeding — such who
bring

Your Majesty's dear reign dishonour.   Thanks,
Friends of Chinon!   Thanks for your keen rebuke.
I know what you would say :   Here stands our King,
Our sacred liege, namesake of Charlemagne,
And we, who take our dignities from him,
And only shine because we are his servants,
Much it becomes us now, in his great need,
To be no more his gossips, chamberlains
And poetasters —

> [*Tearing his parchment.*]

                  but his soldiers.   **Pray,**
Sieur La Tremouille, throw this in the fire :
This is that little rondel on the weather.
[*With emotion, he offers his hand to La Tremouille, who*
refuses it icily.]

LA TREMOUILLE

Your fire will scarce prevent *its raining* still,
If Heaven so wills it, sir.

D'ALENÇON
[*At first feels the repulse keenly, then speaks in quiet disdain.*]
                True, if Heaven wills it.

[*Turning to the hearth, D'Alençon throws the parchment*
into the flames.]

CHARLES
[*Giving him his hand, diffidently.*]
D'Alençon — thanks !

LA TREMOUILLE
[*To De Chartres.*]
                Our scrimmage now is on.
Let see which wins.

ATHENIE

The duke was warm.

CATHERINE

La! Let

Our little King still dream his name is France.
Sure, he will soon believe this milking-maid
Who comes to crown him.

ATHENIE

Milking-maid?

CATHERINE

Why, she

Who rode in town the eve of yesterday,
The soldier-shepherdess, — Jeanne la Pucelle,
The people call her.

LA TREMOUILLE

The dear people love

To label any peasant drab a "virgin,"
And every charlatan a "shepherdess."

LA HIRE

Tonnerre de dieu! What man hath seen the face
Of Jeanne the Maid and named her charlatan?
Her face — God's eyes! When I am cooked and
damn'd,
And devils twirl me on a spit in hell,
I'll think upon that face and have redemption.

D'ALENÇON

[*Who has listened with eager interest.*]

Then you have seen her?

LA HIRE

> Once, and ever since
My fingers have been itching at my sword
To crack an English skull and win her smile.

DIANE

O miracles! Monsieur the Growler speaks
In praise of women.

CATHERINE

> Ah, my love, but think
How man's gear doth become the maiden shape.

LA HIRE
[To La Tremouille.]

And if she be not white as maidenhood,
I will — before these ladies and your Grace —
Pluck out mine eye-teeth.

LA TREMOUILLE

> Save them, sir; 'tis plain
She hath already plucked your wisdom out.
> *[Deliberately.]*
I do not love this Jeanne.

LA HIRE
[Bowing.]
> I do, Seigneur.

ATHENIE
[With awe, aside to Diane.]
He'd better have drunk poison than said that.

D'ALENÇON

Marshal La Hire, your hand! Fame hath described
    you —
Your pardon! — as a rake-hell, hydrophobious
Gascon, who bites at all men —

       [Glancing at La Tremouille.]

                  even favourites.
I pray, sir, as the fire regales the hearth-mouse,
Grant me your friendship.

LA HIRE
[Giving his hand.]
           Sir, you have it — hot.

D'ALENÇON

This Jeanne the Maid, you think she is — inspired?

LA HIRE

No, sir! — I *know* it.

D'ALENÇON
[With a faint, indulgent smile.]
         This will interest
His Majesty: pray, will you tell him more?

LA TREMOUILLE
[Watching D'Alençon escort La Hire to Charles.]
By God, the man usurps me.

DE CHARTRES
            But I thought
You laid an ambush for this charlatan
To keep her from the King.

F

LA TREMOUILLE

        The plan failed.   Now
She is quartered here within the castle tower.
The doctors of Poitiers are with her there,
Cross-questioning her faith and sanity.

DE CHARTRES

Will, then, the King receive her?

LA TREMOUILLE

        He must not.
No; from this castle's tower she must depart
Back to Lorraine.

    [*Indicating D'Alençon and La Hire.*]

        These babblers must be hushed,
And Jeanne's reception foiled. Such sparks make
    flames.
Already she hath kindled the people; soon
She might inflame the King himself to action;
Then — follow me! If France *should* whip the
    English,
Charles would be solvent.

DE CHARTRES

        And you really fear
Lest one weak girl shall overturn the world?

LA TREMOUILLE

One should *fear* nothing; what one *knows* is this:
'Well for oneself is well enough for the world.'
In short, at present all is well for *me*.

D'ALENÇON

[*To Vendôme, who has entered and spoken with him.*]
Bring here the men ; they shall be very welcome.

LA HIRE

Our livers are too fat, your Majesty.
We Frenchmen are a herd of potted geese
A *paté de fois gras* to cram the bellies
Of British mongrels.

CHARLES

Still, sir,—

LA HIRE

Ventre du diable !

Flanders, Artois, Champagne, and Picardy,
Normandy — gobbled, all of 'em ! And now
Talbot, the English mastiff, with his whelps,
Squats on his haunch and howls at Orleans' gate,
And Scales and Suffolk bark around the walls.
God's bones ! and what do we ? Seize up our cudgels
And drive the curs back to their island-kennel ?
Nay, sire, we scare 'em off with nursery-songs.

CHARLES

You speak your mind a little harshly, Marshal ?

LA HIRE

I keep but one about me, sire, and that
Is likely to go off in people's noses
Like this new brand of snuff called gunpowder.

[*To a servant who has come to him from La Tremouille.*]
His grace would wish to speak with me ?— Delighted !
[*He follows the servant to La Tremouille, who speaks aside
to him.*]

CHARLES

[*Utterly dejected by La Hire's words.*]

What can I do, D'Alençon? I am pawned
And patched and mortgaged to my finger-nails.
The very turnspits in the kitchen whistle
For wages at me, and I bid them whistle.
What can I do but *play* at King?

D'ALENÇON

A change
Of policy would bring you instant funds.
Your people would recover your lost cities,
If you would captain them.

CHARLES

My people! Ah!
'Tis God alone could make this people mine,
By consecrated rite and taintless seed
From sire to royal son. I had a mother,
Who left me for her royal legacy
A monstrous doubt in a tiny syllable:
Legitimate or *il*legitimate? —
Cure me *that* ill, and I will conquer Europe.

D'ALENÇON

Boethius saith, there is one antidote
To being born; that is — philosophy.

LA HIRE

[*To La Tremouille.*]

Excuse me, sir! This silence is too golden
For me to keep it by me. I have heard,

When I was hatched, the mid-wife split my tongue
And had me suckled by a certain jackdaw,
That was the village wet-nurse. — Who can vouch
For all one hears?

LA TREMOUILLE

Silence must come to all:
To some a little sooner. — I have said.

LA HIRE
[Bowing.]

As soon as God shall have your Grace's permit,
I shall be ready! (*Lower*) Yet I warn your Grace,
Bury me not too shallow under sod,
Lest, where the stink is, *other* jackdaws scratch
And cause your Grace's nose embarrassment.
[*Reënter Vendôme, followed by* DE METZ *and* DE POULANGY, *whom he escorts to D'Alençon and Charles.*]

D'ALENÇON

Your name?

DE METZ

Mine: Jean de Metz, servant of France.

D'ALENÇON

And yours?

DE POULANGY

Bertrand de Poulangy.

D'ALENÇON
[To both.]

Your master?

DE METZ

Robert de Baudricourt of Vaucouleurs.

CHARLES

He sent you to conduct this shepherdess
Here to our castle ?

DE METZ

And beseech you, King,
To give her audience.

D'ALENÇON

You travelled shrewdly
To escape the English and Burgundians.
They hold the river-bridges and the fords.

DE METZ

We escaped by miracle : at black of night,
We swam our horses through the swollen streams;
At dawn, we couched in hiding; at our side
She slept all day in armour; and we prayed.
It was the Maid who brought us safely here.

D'ALENÇON

Nay, but you say you were in hiding.

DE METZ

Yet
It was the Maid ; she said it should be so.

D'ALENÇON

Can she, then, prophesy ?

DE METZ

She is from God.

D'ALENÇON
[*Smiling.*]

You told us — from Lorraine !

DE METZ

Even so from God.
Out of Lorraine, beside the Ladies' Tree,
Shall come a maid — saviour of France.

CHARLES

What's that?

D'ALENÇON

A legend old as Merlin.

LA TREMOUILLE
[*Who has approached.*]

And as heathen.
[*To De Metz and De Poulangy.*]
You are dismissed.

DE METZ
[*To Charles.*]

Beseech your Majesty
To grant her audience!

DE POULANGY

She is from God.

DE CHARTRES

That shall the judgment of the Church decide.

LA TREMOUILLE

The door is open.

DE METZ
[*Supplicatingly.*]
Gracious King!

CHARLES

But George —

LA TREMOUILLE

Don't fear; the beggars shall not plague thee, boy.

CHARLES

Nay, by St. Denis! but they plague me not.
A March-mad peasant-wench will pass the time.
I'll see the lass.

LA TREMOUILLE

Good-nature kills thee, Charles.

[*Dismissing De Metz and De Poulangy with a gesture.*]
His Majesty regrets —

D'ALENÇON

His Majesty
Regrets he might not sooner speak with her.
[*To the Chamberlain.*]
Vendôme, go with these men, and tell the Maid
The King will see her now.

LA TREMOUILLE

[*Eying D'Alençon with shrewd defiance.*]
Sir, is this wise?

D'ALENÇON

Whether 'tis wise, your Grace, depends perhaps
Whether one holds a first or second mortgage.
Foreclosure of a second might be folly.
[*A slight pause.*]

LA TREMOUILLE

What's this — a parable?

D'ALENÇON

     Why, what you please;
Call it a hook and line. I knew a man
Who turned fish-monger of an Easter eve.

LA TREMOUILLE
[*With a piqued smile and shrug.*]
Nonsense prevails!
[*As De Metz and De Poulangy go out, he turns aside to De Chartres.*]
     The devil fetch this duke!
I would I knew what he hath loaned to Charles.

CHARLES
[*Pensively.*]
"Out of Lorraine, beside the Ladies' Tree,
Shall come a maid — saviour of France." — D'Alen-
 çon!
What if this wench, green from her vines and cheeses,
Her sheep-shears and her spindle, should dispel
My sovereign doubt. — Nay, listen! If she be
From God indeed, and I be truly King,
She should detect my royal sanctity
Under what guise soever; ought she not?

D'ALENÇON
There are some powers of nature little known.
But what may be your plan?

CHARLES
     I say, unless
She be a charlatan, or I base-born,
She'll recognize me by her holy vision
As King amongst a thousand.

LA TREMOUILLE
[*Eagerly.*]
                          That must follow,
Of course.

D'ALENÇON
          I think it follows not; but, sire,
What means of testing —

CHARLES
                    This!   She comes but newly
From far Lorraine, hath never seen my face,
Nor heard my voice, nor set foot in this hall.
Good!   You and I, D'Alençon, shall change cloaks,
You shall be King — she hath not seen thee?

D'ALENÇON
                                        Never.

CHARLES
Good!   I will be D'Alençon and stand here
One of the court, subordinate, whilst you
Sit yonder on the throne-chair — Charles of France.
Then let her enter.

LA TREMOUILLE
                    Bravo, Charles!   A plot
Of genius!

CHARLES
          Nay, a pleasant ruse.

D'ALENÇON
                              But if
She fail to uncloak the counterfeit?   Such slips
Are common to the best of us.

CHARLES

At least
We shall have killed an hour in a new way,
And one less hoax to trouble us.

VENDÔME
[*Announces at the door.*]

The Maid!
The reverend masters are conducting her
Here to your Majesty.

CHARLES

Be quick, D'Alençon!
[*As Charles, stripping off his outer garment, reaches it to
D'Alençon, La Tremouille beckons Vendôme to himself.*]

D'ALENÇON
[*Hesitating.*]

You wish it, sire?

CHARLES

At once.
[*They exchange cloaks, but the placard of King Dagobert is
discarded to a servant.*]

LA TREMOUILLE
[*To Vendôme, indicating to him the fact of the exchange.*]

You understand.
[*Exit Vendôme.*]
[*With an exultant smile, to De Chartres.*]
This whim of Charles's relieves us of much pains.
Look where he prays to the glass emperor.

[*La Tremouille points at Charles, who — wearing D'Alençon's cloak of dun — stands beneath the window of
stained glass, and supplicates it, apart.*]

CHARLES

Thou, Charlemagne, dead sire and mighty saint!
If in my veins thy hallowed blood still runs,
Let through this mean disguise thy royal spirit shine,
And make, in me, thy race and honour manifest.

[*D'Alençon, wearing Charles's royal cloak, sits on the throne.
All those present range themselves as his subjects, some
standing near, others closing about Charles, where he
stands (right centre).*

Reënter then, at back, Vendôme, followed by DOCTORS
*of the Church; these by De Metz and De Poulangy,
who stand by the door; last enters Jeanne, dressed as a
man. The Doctors, exchanging with Vendôme a hardly
detectable look of understanding, approach D'Alençon,
make their obeisances, and stand away. Vendôme,
motioning then to Jeanne, moves forward to conduct her
to D'Alençon as king, but pauses as she does not follow.
Standing in the doorway, Jeanne, lifting her face in-
tensely toward the stained-glass window, seems to listen.
At the same moment, while the eyes of all are centred
upon Jeanne, there emerges from the great fireplace,
where logs are burning, and stands upon the hearth
with flaming wings, St. Michael, who gazes also at
Jeanne. The only sound or other motion in the hall
is caused by the Court-fool, who, springing up from the
throne-footstool to whisper of the Maid in D'Alençon's
ear, sets thereby the bells on his cap to tinkling silverly.
Simultaneously, the voice of St. Catherine speaks, as
from mid-air.*]

THE VOICE

Daughter of God, choose boldly.

[*Glancing slowly through the hall, the eyes of Jeanne meet
those of St. Michael, who points with his hand at*

Charles, then turns and disappears within the smoke and glow of the fireplace. Moving then with decision, Jeanne follows Vendôme, but oblivious of D'Alençon, passes on straight to Charles, before whom she kneels down.]

JEANNE

Gentle Dauphin,
My name is Jeanne the Maid, and I am come
To bring you tidings from the King of Heaven
That He by means of me shall consecrate
And crown you King at Rheims.
[*The hall remains silent and awed. Charles is visibly moved.*]

CHARLES

I am not the King.

JEANNE

Truly you are the Dauphin — Charles of France,
Who shall be King when God anointeth you
In His cathedral.

D'ALENÇON

By my fay, young maid,
Thou dost not flatter us with homage. Rise
And stand before us. *We* are Charles of France.

JEANNE

I rise, Seigneur, but not unto the King.
You are not Charles of France.

DE CHARTRES
[*With emotion, aside to La Tremouille.*]
This troubles me.

LA TREMOUILLE
[*Caustically.*]

We have been tricked somewhere.

D'ALENÇON

'Tis plain, good Jeanne,
That thou art wandered in some winter's tale,
Wherein lèse-majesté to fairy-princes
Doth little matter.   You are smiling ?   What
Do we remind you on ?

JEANNE
[*Meeting his mood.*]

In truth, Seigneur,
At home in Domremy where I was born
There lives an old good-wife, who used to tell
How Master Donkey wore King Lion's mane.

LA HIRE
[*Exploding in laughter.*]

Tonnerre !

JEANNE
[*Changing instantly.*]

Nay, honourable lords, and you
Fair gentlewomen, truly am I come
Into your midst — a sheep-maid dull and rude.
Pass on ! Of that no more.   But which of you
Hath cunning to deceive the sight of God ?
Or which would speak a lie unto his Lord ?
My Lord hath sent me here, His messenger,
But He hath girt me with a thousand more
Whose eyes are many as the nesting birds

And voices as cicadas in the summer.
Lo! in this hall they hover o'er you now,
But your dissembling eyes send up a mist
To obscure their shining wings.   O gentles, mock
No more, but show God your true faces!

[*A pause, filled with the various pantomime of uneasiness,
admiration, and wonder.   All look for decision to
D'Alençon.*]

D'ALENÇON

[*Rising abruptly, comes down.*]

Maid,

I lied to you.   I am the Duke d'Alençon.

JEANNE

Dearer to France as duke than King, Seigneur.

[*She extends to him her hand — strong, peasantly, with a
frank smile.   He takes it, amazed, and unconsciously
continues to hold it.*]

CHARLES

[*Exultant, seizes La Tremouille's shoulder.*]

She knew me, George!   Unswervingly, at once,
In spite of all our cunning. —

LA TREMOUILLE

Hm!

CHARLES

She knew me;

George! but you saw.

LA TREMOUILLE

These charlatans are shrewd.

CHARLES

What? — What!

LA TREMOUILLE
I cannot say.

CHARLES
But you beheld,
Behold!
LA TREMOUILLE
It may be. — I have heard — who knows
What hidden conspirator — Satan perhaps.

CHARLES
Satan!
LA TREMOUILLE
Why not?
CHARLES
[*Aside, imploringly.*]
D'Alençon, question her!
What deem *you* of this proof? What *is* this maid?
[*D'Alençon, having started at being addressed, has released Jeanne's hand.*]

D'ALENÇON
I know not, sire. — 'Tis that which fascinates me.
[*Looking again at Jeanne with his former friendly puzzled look, he hesitates, then speaks, embarrassed. Throughout the following brief scene — stirred by mingled mystification and admiration of the peasant girl— he, in his questioning, halts occasionally; in which gaps La Tremouille steps shrewdly in.*]

D'ALENÇON
Jeanne d'Arc, you have well stood — or *seemed* to stand —
Our playful ruse — his Majesty's and mine —
To test your boasted powers.

JEANNE
[*Simply.*]
I have no powers
To boast, Seigneur.

D'ALENÇON
You have been catechised
Already by these reverend Doctors here?

JEANNE
Since dawn they have not ceased to question me.

D'ALENÇON
What is your verdict thus far, Master Seguin?

SEGUIN
Your Grace, we find no fault in her.

LA TREMOUILLE
[*Aside to De Chartres.*]
Come, come;
Now *you* are needed.

DE CHARTRES
[*Aside, moved with confusion.*]
I believe in her.

LA TREMOUILLE
Our privy council fails us now?

DE CHARTRES
Her face!

LA TREMOUILLE
[*Acidly.*]
Pardieu!

G

D'ALENÇON
[*To Jeanne.*]

What is this boon which you have come
To beg his Majesty ?

JEANNE
I beg, Seigneur,
A troop of the good fighting men of France,
That I may lead them, by the help of God,
To drive from France the wicked Englishmen
That 'siege his town of Orleans.

LA HIRE
[*Striding back and forth.*]

Sacré bleu!
Boil 'em in peppermint.

LA TREMOUILLE
[*To Jeanne, intervening, as D'Alençon gazes in admiration.*]

Most excellent !
That thou, a shepherd lass, shouldst leave thy wool
To instruct our captains in the craft of war.

JEANNE
My Lord hath willed it so.

LA TREMOUILLE
Who is thy lord ?

JEANNE
The King of Heaven that is the King of France
Till He shall crown the Dauphin.

D'ALENÇON

[*To La Tremouille.*]

Sir, your pardon :
I am now catechiser. — Slowly, Jeanne :
If God hath willed to bring deliverance
To France, then soldiers are superfluous.
Why do you ask for soldiers ?

JEANNE

En nom Dé !

The soldiers are to fight, and God to give
The victory.

[*Murmurs of approbation.*]

D'ALENÇON

You do not then believe
In God His power ?

JEANNE

[*Gravely.*]

Better than you, Seigneur.

D'ALENÇON

[*At first amused, then strangely moved by this character-reading, drops again the thread of his questioning in self-revery.*]

Better than I !

[*He continues to watch and listen to Jeanne, absorbed in her
as in some problem unsolved.*]

LA TREMOUILLE

You have observed, my friends,
The circling orbit of these arguments,

That veer like swallows round a chimney hole.
Clearly we must await some *valid* sign
Before we trust this maid.

JEANNE

My noble masters!
I come not to Chinon to show you signs,
But give me those good fighters, and for sign
I will deliver Orleans.

LA TREMOUILLE

Have you, then,
No other sign to show?

JEANNE

I have, indeed,
A sign — but not for you.   It may be seen
By one alone, my Dauphin.

CHARLES

Me!   By me?

JEANNE

O gentle Dauphin, by the love you bear
To France, and by the love of France for you,
Hear me — but not with these.

CHARLES
[*To all.*]

Leave us alone.

LA TREMOUILLE
[*Aside.*]

Remember, Charles, what black confederate
Instructs this man-maid.

CHARLES
Let the court withdraw.

LA TREMOUILLE
[*Dryly, to Charles.*]
I stay, my dear!

JEANNE
[*Very quietly, standing with her eyes focussed far.*]
The Seigneur will withdraw.

LA TREMOUILLE
[*Drawing away after the others toward the stairway, over-
takes De Chartres, aside.*]
She is possessed.

DE CHARTRES
By angels.

D'ALENÇON
[*Withdrawing last with La Hire.*]
Friend La Hire,
How much of miracle, think you, do we
Ignore in simple nature?
[*Charles is now left alone with Jeanne, beyond the others'
hearing.*]

CHARLES
Shepherdess,
How knewest thou it was I, among the many?

JEANNE
My Voices said, " Choose boldly," and I knew.

CHARLES
What voices, Jeanne?

JEANNE

You must believe in me
To hear them.

CHARLES

Tell me ; is it known of them
Or thee — this doubt which is my stain and cancer ?

JEANNE

That doubt is as the darkness of the blind
Which *is* not.

CHARLES

[*Feverishly.*]

Is not ? Oh, give me the sign !

JEANNE

You must believe before you may behold.

CHARLES

Look in my eyes, Jeanne ; I begin to see.

JEANNE

My Dauphin must believe ; he shall believe.

CHARLES

[*Sinking to his knees.*]

The crown !

JEANNE

[*Intense.*]

Believe !

CHARLES

He lifts it.

[*The clock begins to chime. In the same instant, the sun-
lit form of the Emperor in the stained glass is seen to*

turn toward the King — where he gazes at him past the face of Jeanne — and to hold out aloft the glowing crown of fleur-de-lis. From the colonnade, the persons of the court look on, whisper together, pointing at the King, where apparently he is kneeling, struck with adoration, at the feet of Jeanne. D'Alençon, standing forward from the rest of the court, is intent upon Jeanne, as, with the inward light of a vision mirrored, her face looks down on the King with a mighty intensity.]

THE EMPEROR IN THE STAINED GLASS
[*Speaks with the voice of St. Michael.*]
Charles the Seventh!
Inheritor of France, legitimate
By birth —

CHARLES
[*Murmurs.*]
Legitimate!

THE EMPEROR
Behold the crown —
The crown of Charlemagne — which thou shalt wear
At Rheims. This is the Maid, whom God hath sent
To bring thy land and thee deliverance.

[*As the chiming ceases, so the vision. Charles — his hands clasped — rises wildly to his feet.*]

CHARLES
Charlemagne! Charlemagne! Thy blood is vindicated.
My lords, this is the Maid of God!

JEANNE

[*Staggering slightly as with faintness, moves toward D' Alen-çon, who comes to her side.*]

I am tired ;
Thy shoulder, friend !

CHARLES

[*Kneels again, his arms upraised to the stained glass.*]

Charlemagne !

D'ALENÇON

[*As Jeanne rests her forehead on his shoulder, speaks to himself dreamily.*]

Why, 'tis a child !

ACT III

ACT III

SCENE: A Meadow before the Walls of Orleans.
May 7, 1429.

In the near background (occupying a large part of the scene)
a green knoll overlooks the not distant river Loire
flowing toward the right, and a part of the city wall,
which sweeps beyond view, left.   On this knoll are dis-
covered Franciscan friars grouped about an altar, be-
side which floats a white painted banner, sprinkled with
fleur-de-lis.[1] *One of these friars,* PIGACHON, *is dressed*
half in armour, his cassock — worn over a steel corslet —
being tucked up, thus revealing his legs encased in steel.
On the left of the scene are women, old men, and priests
of Orleans.   The foreground and the rest of the adjacent
meadow are thronged with French officers and soldiery.
In the midst of the latter (centre), Jeanne d'Arc — in
full armour — is dictating a letter, which PASQUEREL, *her*
confessor, transcribes on a parchment.

---

[1] On one side of this banner (which, authentically, was Jeanne's
personal standard) is depicted — on the ground of fleur-de-lis — Christ
in Glory, holding the world and giving His benediction to a lily, held by
one of two angels, who are kneeling at each side; on the other side
the figure of the Virgin and a shield with the arms of France, sup-
ported by two angels.

The friars also have in their charge two smaller banners, viz.: one
a pennon, on which is represented the Annunciation; the other, a
banneret, adorned with the Crucifixion.

JEANNE

" King of England ; and you, Duke of Bedford,
who call yourself Regent of the Kingdom of France ;
you, William De la Pole, Earl of Suffolk ; John, Lord
Talbot ; and you, Thomas Lord Scales, Lieutenants
of the same duke ; make satisfaction to the King of
Heaven ; give up to the Maid, who is sent hither by
God, the keys of all the good towns in France, which
ye have taken. And as for you, archers, companions-
in-arms, gentlemen, and others who are before this
town of Orleans, get you home to your own country
by God His command ; and if this be not done, then
once more will we come upon you with so great an
ha, ha ! as shall be remembered these thousand years.
Answer now if ye will make peace in this city of
Orleans, which if ye do not, ye may be reminded on,
to your much hurt.

Jhesus Maria — Jehanne la Pucelle."

Good Pasquerel, I know not A nor B ;
Where shall I make my cross ?

PASQUEREL

Here, Angelique.

[*Jeanne makes her cross on the parchment, which she then
rolls tight and ties to an arrow.*]

JEANNE

De Metz, ride to the bridge and shoot this arrow
Across the Loire into the English lines. —
Wait, aim it toward the tower of the Tournelles
Into the conning-shaft where Suffolk stands.

DE METZ

And if they make no answer ?

JEANNE

We have fought
Since daybreak.   We can fight again till dark ;
And after that to-morrow, and to-morrow.
[*Exit De Metz, with the arrow, amid shouts of the people
and soldiers.*]

DUNOIS

Your words are brave, Pucelle, and they are holy;
But holy words are weak against stone walls.
The English fortress is too strong for us.

LA HIRE

Now by the hang'd thieves of Gethsemane !

JEANNE
[*Sternly.*]

Gascon !

LA HIRE

Forgive, my captain : by my stick !
I swear to God I swore but by my stick.
You said a man might curse upon his stick.

JEANNE

You do well to bethink you, Marshal; mind,
Who spits 'gainst Heaven, it falleth on his head.
[*Pulling his ear with her hand.*]
But thou art my brave Growler for all that !
[*Jeanne passes to speak earnestly to other officers.*]

LA HIRE

Now by my stick, Dunois, without offence,
Thou liest in thy windpipe and thy gorge

To say the English walls are made of stone;
And if the Maid of God shall say the word,
By supper-time we'll roll 'em out as flat
As apple-jacks, with English blood for syrup.

DUNOIS

Truly the Maid of God hath wrought strange things
Yet there be bounds —

LA HIRE

　　　　　Eight days! Eight days! Dunois,
Since she set foot in Orleans, and look now!
The enemy that hemmed you in a web
Of twenty fortresses now holds but one.

DUNOIS

But that one — the Tournelles!

LA HIRE

　　　　　　　And think ye, then,
That she who turns French poodles into lions,
And changes British mastiffs into hares,
Will find it difficult to change yon tower
Into a sugar-loaf? I tell thee, man,
She is from God, and doth whatso she will.

JEANNE

[*To D'Alençon, who in his armour stands reading.*]
A book, my knight? And your good sword yet hot?

D'ALENÇON

The war-horse, Jeanne, still craves his manger-oats. —
My book is a little island in the battle,
And I am moored alongside in this lull
To barter with strange natives — deeds, for dreams
Of deeds.

JEANNE

Is it the holy gospel?

D'ALENÇON

No.

JEANNE

Whereof, then, do you read?

D'ALENÇON

Of you, Madonna!
When you were virgin-queen of Attica,
And all your maiden Amazons in arms
Hailed you "Hippolyta."

JEANNE

[*Putting from him the book, hands him his sword with a friendly smile.*]

This is your sword,
My bonny duke; and this dear ground is France.
I know naught of your queens and "anticas."

A PRIEST

[*In the crowd.*]

Jeanne! Jeanne the Maid!

JEANNE

Who calls me?

THE PRIEST

Speak to us —
What of the battle?

SEVERAL VOICES

Tell us! Speak to us!

JEANNE

Good folk, you hearts of Orleans, holy fathers!
What would you that I tell you?

SEVERAL VOICES

Prophesy!

JEANNE

Ah, friends, if you would hear of bloody stars,
Of sun-dogs, and of mare's tails in the dawn,
Go to your gossips and your weather-wives;
'Tis ours to fight and God's to prophesy.
Yet what our Lord hath spoken by His Saints
To me, I speak to you again : be glad,
For not in vain, good men, have you stood strong
And shared your loaves of famine, crumb by crumb,
To man your walls against our wicked foe;
And not in vain, mothers of Orleans, you
Have rocked your cradles by the cannon's side
To bring your sons and husbands ease of sleep;
For you have kept this city for your Lord,
Which is the King of Heaven, and He hath come
To recompense you now.   Therefore, return
Within your gates again, and when you hear,
Thrice blown, upon this horn, God's warning blast,
Then ring your bells for France and victory.

[*To her page.*]

Louis, the horn!

[LOUIS DE CONTES *blows the horn once.*]

So shall you know His sign.

[*The people depart with gestures of benediction and hope.*]

D'ALENÇON

[*Standing with La Hire, near Jeanne.*]

A child! and her clear eyes, upturned to Heaven,
Shall influence the stars of all the ages.

[*Clutching his companion's arm.*]

La Hire! We are living *now*, can watch, can serve her!

LA HIRE

Aye, folk that live in other times are damned.

[*An altar bell sounds.*]

PIGACHON

[*To Jeanne.*]

The Vespers, Angelique.

JEANNE

Soldiers, the Mass!
And let all you that have confessed yourselves
This day, kneel down, and let the rest depart
Until confession.

[*All kneel, save some few, who depart, abashed. Among
these is D'Alençon, whom Jeanne stays wistfully.*]

You, my duke?

D'ALENÇON

I am
A tardy Christian, Jeanne.

JEANNE

I pray you kneel
Beside me. My good Pasquerel will hear you.

[*D'Alençon kneels beside Jeanne and Pasquerel; Pigachon
among the friars is about to conduct the service at the*

*altar, when De Metz's voice is heard calling (off right),
and he enters, followed immediately by an English Herald, who, bearing himself defiant, holds in his hand a
parchment.*]

DE METZ

Jeanne ! — Maid of God !

THE ENGLISH HERALD
Where is the whore of France ?

[*The kneeling soldiers start up in turbulence.*]

SOLDIERS

La Mort !   La Mort !

JEANNE
[*Keeping them back.*]
Peace !   Let the herald speak ;
His privilege is sacred.   (*To D'Alençon*)   Stop them.

HERALD
Where
Is she who calls herself the Maid of God ?

JEANNE
I am the Maid.

HERALD
[*Speaking, but at times referring with his eyes to the parch-
ment.*]
Thus saith my Lord, the King
Of England, by his servant Suffolk, Captain
Before the walls of Orleans : Whore of France —

D'ALENÇON
Death ! —

JEANNE

[*Clings to him.*]

Stay! He speaks not for himself, but Suffolk;
His cloth is holy.

D'ALENÇON

[*Bitterly.*]

Holy!

HERALD

Courtesan
Of him who shames the blood of Charlemagne,
Consort of Satan, which hast ta'en the limbs
And outward seeming of a peasant wench
To execute thy damnèd sorceries
On England's sons, to please thy paramour —

JEANNE

[*To the soldiers, who grow more clamorous.*]

Yet patience, *garçons* !

HERALD

Thou unvirgin thing,
Which art vaingloried in the garb of man ;
Thou impudent, thou subtle, thou unclean —

JEANNE

[*Choking back the tears.*]

No, no! Thou hast forgot what thou shouldst say !

HERALD

Thus fling we back thy poison'd script unread,
And therewith this defiance : Work thy worst,
And with the hand of strange paralysis

H

Strike numb with fear our noble English host;
Yet shall we still resist thee with our souls,
And in the day when Christ shall let thee fall
Within our power, then shalt thou make amends
In fire for all thy witchcraft, and in fire
Shall thy unhallow'd spirit return to hell.

D'ALENÇON

Hold, gentlemen! Wait yet if he have done
This "holy privilege" of infamy.

HERALD

Sir, I am done.
[*D'Alençon, taking the little pennon of the Annunciation
from a friar, hands it to the Herald.*]

D'ALENÇON

Take, then, this back with you
In token who it is whom you profane.
Lock it within your fortress' strongest tower,
And tell your masters that a simple maid
Of France shall fetch it home, this night, to Orleans.
[*Exit Herald with pennon. The soldiers mutter applause
and execrations.*]

JEANNE

[*Hiding her face, turns to D'Alençon.*]
What have I done that they should name me so?

LA HIRE

Par mon baton! We'll answer them in blood.

DUNOIS

Your places, officers!

JEANNE

[*Starts to Pigachon and the soldiers.*]

The psalm! Your psalm!

[*Pigachon and the friars raise the chant of the hymn of Charlemagne. This is immediately taken up by all the soldiers, who, under its influence, pass out in solemn enthusiasm, led by D'Alençon and Jeanne, the latter carrying in her hand the banneret with the Crucifixion.*]

ALL

Veni creator spiritus,
Mentes tuorum visita,
Imple superna gratia
Quæ tu creasti pectora.

[*There now remain behind only Pasquerel and the Franciscan friars, grouped around Jeanne's standard of the fleur-de-lis. These continue the chant in a low tone, as the voices of the soldiers grow fainter in the distance.*]

FRIARS

Qui paraclitus diceris
Donum Dei altissimi
Fons vivus, ignis, caritas
Et spiritalis unctio.

Hostem repellas longius
Pacemque dones protinus,
Ductore sic te prævio
Vitemus omne noxium.

[*During the last verses Pasquerel, having examined the banner critically, fetches a copper box, opens it, lays out some sewing and painting materials, lowers the banner,*] *and bends over it solicitously. With the last words of the chant, a serene quiet falls upon the knoll, save when, from time to time, contrasting sounds of the distant battle interrupt, or fill the pauses of the conversation between Pasquerel and Pigachon.*]

PASQUEREL

Reach me my palette yonder, Pigachon.
Our Lord hath something scathed his brow and lip
I' the last mêlée, and one of his white lilies
Is smirched with river-slime.   Take you my needle
And hem this ravell'd edge, whilst I retouch
The Saviour's robe and face.

PIGACHON
                    The crimson silk
Or white?
                    PASQUEREL
            The white is better for the hem.
Now for our Lord, what say you? — to the lip
A touch of *Garence rose?*   I much prefer
Myself, for blush and richness of the blood,
A *Garence rose dorée* to cinnabar ;
Yet thereof Master Fra Angelico
Of Florence might be critical.

PIGACHON
[*Threading his needle.*]
                    May be.
PASQUEREL

Well, masters think not two alike.
            [*Giving a touch.*]
                    Voilà !

[*Silence, and the distant battle.*]

Saw you the mauve and pink geraniums
In Brother Michel's hot-bed?

PIGACHON
                    Wonderful!

PASQUEREL

He waters them at prime and curfew.

PIGACHON
                              Ha!
[*Silence again; the two friars work on.*]

PASQUEREL
[*Suddenly.*]

I have it, Pigachon! It comes to me!
To touch this lily's petal-tips with rose
In token that it bleeds.

PIGACHON
                    Why does it bleed?

PASQUEREL

But thou art mule-brain'd, Pigachon. Know, then,
It bleeds for sorrow of its little sisters,
The fleur-de-lis of France, because they lie
Bleeding and trampled by the fiends of England.

PIGACHON

Ah!

PASQUEREL

Yet perchance the Maid might disapprove.

PIGACHON

May be.

PASQUEREL

[*Sighs.*]

Well, well ; I will not make it bleed.

[*Enter, amid louder cries from the battle, Louis de Contes with two men, fettered.*]

LOUIS

Your name ?

THE FIRST MAN

John Gris, Knight to the King of England.

LOUIS

Yours ?

THE OTHER

Adam Goodspeed, yeoman.

LOUIS

John Gris, Knight,

And Adam Goodspeed, yeoman, you are bound
As prisoners to Louis, called De Contes,
Page to God's maiden Jeanne, called La Pucelle.

GRIS

Sith God hath dropped us in the Devil's clutch,
His will be done.

GOODSPEED

Amen.

PASQUEREL

[*Springing up from his paints, stares off scene (right), appalled.*]

O dolorosa !

[*Enter D'Alençon, supporting Jeanne, and followed by La Hire and a group of soldiers.*]

D'ALENÇON

Go back, La Hire : let not this thing be known.
[*Exeunt La Hire and soldiers.*]

JEANNE

Where is my standard ? Rest me here.

D'ALENÇON

             The gates
Are but a little farther.

JEANNE

        In God's name
I will not leave the field. — My standard !
[*She sinks down beside it.*]

D'ALENÇON
[*To Louis.*]
           Run !
Fetch from the town a litter.
[*To Pasquerel.*]
          Have you oil ?
Prepare a heated compress for the wound ;
She is stricken and may die.

[*Louis, after fastening his prisoners to a log (left), departs
with a friar. Pasquerel, after lighting a charcoal
brazier, begins with D'Alençon's help to tear and fold a
bandage.*]

JEANNE
[*Faintly.*]
        Good Pigachon !
PIGACHON
You called me, Angelique ?

JEANNE

                    Go to my men
And tell them I am well.

PIGACHON
[*Dubious.*]
                    A lie ?

JEANNE
                                        A little,
A white lie : God will make of it a star
To shine on Orleans when she is delivered.

PIGACHON

I go.

            [*Exit right.*]

PASQUEREL
[*Looking after him.*]
Would *I* might tell a lie for her !

JEANNE

No, dear my bonny duke, you shall not touch ;
I'll pluck it out myself.

D'ALENÇON

                    Thou must not, Jeanne ;
The barb hath sunken deep ; thou art but a girl.

JEANNE

I am a soldier. — Think you it will bleed ?
Ah, Heaven, if it should bleed !

D'ALENÇON
[*As Jeanne, turning away, clutches at her side.*]
                            What dost thou ?

JEANNE

See,
There is the arrow.   I will keep my eyes
A little shut —

D'ALENÇON

She's dying, Pasquerel;
She's torn the arrow forth with her own hand.
Help me to bear her to the city gate.

PASQUEREL

She said beside her standard.

D'ALENÇON

But, thou sot
Of superstition, she is dying.   Are
Her wishes dearer to thee than her life?

PASQUEREL

She is from God.

D'ALENÇON

O idiotic phrase!
We soldiers babble it like paraquets,
And let a child — this brave and dreamy girl —
Die in the sacrifice for us — for us!
Jeanne, thou must live — Jeanne! Though all France
    shall find
Perdition, *thou* must live!

PASQUEREL

Unholy words!
She lives for France.

D'ALENÇON
[*Eagerly, as Jeanne lifts her head.*]
She lives; it is enough!

JEANNE

[*Faintly to D'Alençon.*]

Good neighbour, say to him I had to come.

D'ALENÇON

To whom?

JEANNE

My father.   You will tell him?

D'ALENÇON

Truly.

JEANNE

You know, we have two fathers; one's in heaven.
We must obey the greater. — Was he angry?

D'ALENÇON

I think he was not angry.

JEANNE

That is strange;
His scowl is terrible, and yet he loves us:
My brother Pierre and me the most, I think.
What did he do the day I went away?

D'ALENÇON

Dost thou not know me, Jeanne?

JEANNE

I know thee well.

Thou art the face that comes to my closed eyes,
And in the darkness there I speak to it. —
I knew my mother she would understand,
For often I told her how my Voices said
That I must crown the King, and she would smile,
But always Papa Jacques he scowled.

D'ALENÇON

                                Now gently;
Rest back upon my arm; this is thy friend
D'Alençon. — So!

[Pasquerel and D'Alençon put upon her the compress.]

JEANNE

                My mother hurts me here.
They said it was an arrow in my side,
But I knew well it was the homesickness,
And so I plucked it out, and gave 't to him
My Lord, because it had no business there.

D'ALENÇON

To me you gave it, Jeanne, not to your Lord.

JEANNE

And are you not His knight whom God hath sent
To be my shield in battle? — Verily
I leaned upon your shoulder at Chinon
When I was weary and the world grew dim. —
Thou art D'Alençon and my bonny duke.

[Reënter (left) Louis and the friar with a litter.]

D'ALENÇON

I am your servant, and must bear you now
Back to the town.

DISTANT CRIES

                La Pucelle! Au secours!

JEANNE

You hear!   I cannot go.   They call for me.
Fetch me my horse.

D'ALENÇON

Madonna, you may die.

JEANNE

I may not die before I have performed
My Lord's commandment; they have told me so.

D'ALENÇON

Who told?

JEANNE

My Voices.

D'ALENÇON

Jeanne, for love of France
And truth and thy dear soul, lose not thy life
For vanities and whisperings of the air.

JEANNE

Know you whereof you speak?

D'ALENÇON

I speak of nothing,
For they are naught.

JEANNE

My holy counsel — naught!

D'ALENÇON

Do not believe them, Jeanne.   They are delusions.
Forgive me!   I must speak the truth to save
Thy life.

JEANNE

If this were true, O better death!
But listen!

[*The Franciscans about the altar are beginning to move it
from the knoll to the level ground (on the left).*]

D'ALENÇON
[*Persuadingly, bending near her.*]
Come now with me.   Be a good girl.

JEANNE
Listen, my duke.

D'ALENÇON
'Tis but a friar, bearing
The altar bell.

A VOICE
[*Speaks with the bell, which sounds momentarily as the friar
moves it.*]
Daughter of God, be strong.

JEANNE
[*Gazing before her into Pasquerel's lighted brazier.*]
It is her voice; it is St. Catherine.
See in the little flames how small she shines
And flutters like a moth mid peonies.
But holy saints fear not to singe their wings
In fire.   You see, she is not frightened.

PASQUEREL
[*Sinks, murmuring, to his knees.*]
Pater,
Sanctum sit nomen tuum.

GOODSPEED
[*To Gris.*]
Turn thine eyes
Away!   The witch beginneth her hell charms.

JEANNE
[*Rising to her feet.*]
Thou dear St. Catherine, I will be strong!

PASQUEREL

[*To D'Alençon.*]

And will you now believe?

D'ALENÇON

This is a strength
Unnatural, a fever from the wound.
Jeanne —

JEANNE

Look, D'Alençon, look, they leave the bridge!
Our men have turned.   Alas!   They are beaten back.

[*Enter La Hire, beside himself.*]

LA HIRE

[*Raising both arms to heaven.*]

Lord God, I pray Thee, do Thou for La Hire
What he would do for Thee, if he were God,
And Thou, God, wert La Hire!

D'ALENÇON

What news, and quickly!

LA HIRE

News for the rats and skunks of Europe!   News
For dancing apes and Master Rigadoons!
Dunois himself hath bade our men retreat,
And me, La Hire, to tell it!

CRIES

[*Outside (right).*]

To the gates!

JEANNE

[*Looking toward the battle.*]

Dunois, Dunois, thou hast offended me.

CRIES

[*Outside.*]

The gates !

D'ALENÇON

Our men — they come. — Jeanne, you will fall.
Stay ! — I will rally them.

JEANNE

[*Climbing faintly the knoll, as D'Alençon comes to her support.*]

Still be my shield.

[*Enter Dunois and the French soldiery, in rout.*]

CRIES

The gates of Orleans !

JEANNE

[*From the knoll, speaking from D'Alençon's arms, which uphold her, stays the rout.*]

Halt !

CRIES

The Maid !   The Maid !

JEANNE

Who hath commanded you this thing ?

DUNOIS

Jeanne d'Arc,

The English fortress is impregnable.

JEANNE

Dunois, heaven's fortress is impregnable
By souls of gentlemen who turn their backs.

DUNOIS

You fell; we saw how you were wounded, Maid.

JEANNE

And ye beheld not One who did not fall:
Shame, captains of France! Have ye not heard
" Better a dog's head than a lion's tail " ?
Back to the bridge and show your teeth again!
Back to the bridge and show to God your eyes!

SOLDIERS

Back to the bridge!

JEANNE

My banner, dear my duke!
Come, we will go together, hand in hand. —
Children of France, behold your fleur-de-lis!
Thou, Louis, stay, and when thou shalt have seen
This banner touch the English walls — thy horn!
Blow it at Orleans' gate : the siege is raised!
Follow your lilies now, brave boys of France!
Your lilies! Christ the Lord doth captain you.
Ten thousand of his host surround us. See!
The sun goes down through archings of their wings,
The river burns and eddies with their swords.
Work, work, and God will work! Follow the lilies
And shoot your arrows straight. —*Jhesus-Maria!*

SOLDIERS

Jhesus-Maria! — St. Denis! La France!

[*Exeunt all but Louis de Contes, in the foreground* (*right*),
*and the two English prisoners tied, on the left, below the
knoll. The Franciscans have been led away by Pasquerel toward the town, carrying with them the altar.*]

GRIS

I looked long in her face.   Gentle it seemed
And beautiful.

GOODSPEED

So did the serpent's seem
In Adam's garden.   Oh, the fiend is wise,
And in a witch's face most damnèd fair.

GRIS

Indeed, the spell of her is strange upon me.
[*To Louis.*]
Where is her banner now?

LOUIS

I cannot see;
The low sun hurts my eyes; which way I look
It stares me like a monstrous waning moon
Winked on the blood-red clouds of rolling dust.

GOODSPEED

More like it be the many-headed face
Of Satan mocking us.

LOUIS

The lilies, there!
The Maid!   The Maid!

I

GRIS

What! do we drive her back?

LOUIS

She drives you from the bridge.   Her armour!—
    Now—
Oh, she is blown about and fluttered o'er
By clouds of little golden butterflies,
And where she thrusts her lilied banner through,
She glitters double — in the air and river.

GOODSPEED

Her fiends are blown up from the underworld
To succour her.

GRIS

[*Kneeling.*]

This spell upon me!

LOUIS

                                    Ah!
They hurl you from the drawbridge.   Christ!   You
    drown.
Yonder her banner and the fleur-de-lis!
The Maid hath touched the walls.   *Vive la France!*

[*Rushing up the knoll, Louis turns toward Orleans and
    winds his horn three times.   In an instant, from the
    left, a clamour of horns and shouts and bells reply.
    Away, on the right, the iron din of the battle is still
    heard.   Behind the knoll's outline burns the bright red
    of sunset; against that, raising his horn, stands out
    the tense, lithe silhouette of the little page.*]

ACT FOURTH, SCENE I: JEANNE'S TENT NEAR TROYES; NIGHT

ACT IV

ACT IV

SCENE I: Before the walls of Troyes. July 5, 1429. Night.

On the left (up scene), partly surrounded by cypress trees,
the entrance of a pavilion-like tent (extending off scene,
left) is closed by a mediæval tapestry. At centre, beneath
the trees, stand two benches of wood, one higher than
the other. On the right, a stack of arms, and behind
that vague outlines of a camp. Throughout the scene's
action, from time to time, officers and guards of the
French army pass by, or are visible in their battle-gear,
as portions of the scene. After the rising of the moon,
the walls and towers of the town are dimly visible in
the background.

Enter, right, La Tremouille and CAUCHON, *the latter in the*
garb of a layman.

LA TREMOUILLE

That is her tent; those reddish stars, that move,
Are sentries on the city ramparts. Troyes
Still shuts its gates against the Maid, the last
To stand between Charles and his crown at Rheims.

CAUCHON

He *will* be crowned?

LA TREMOUILLE

We hope yet to prevent.
You heard me speak of Brother Richard, here,

Staying in Troyes.   He is a preaching friar,
A kind of mendicant Demosthenes
Who holds the keys of power between his teeth,
And locks or opes the city with his tongue.
To-night he is coming to interview the Maid
To ascertain whether she be from God.
On that the town's surrender will depend.

CAUCHON

So then —?

LA TREMOUILLE

I think I have forestalled the Maid.
A certain Catherine de la Rochelle —
But never mind.   *Our* point is this : that you
Stand ready, when I will, to yield Jeanne d'Arc
Into the English hands, to burn for witchcraft.

CAUCHON

To burn by course of law.

LA TREMOUILLE
[*Smiling.*]
By law, of course !
[*Enter at back De Chartres, followed by* FLAVY.]

DE CHARTRES
[*Investigating with a torch.*]

Your Grace ?

LA TREMOUILLE
[*To Cauchon.*]

Ah, 'tis our man.
[*To De Chartres.*]
You've brought him ?

DE CHARTRES
[*Revealing Flavy.*]

There.

LA TREMOUILLE

Here is our honest bishop from Beauvais,
Pierre Cauchon.

CAUCHON
[*Indicating his disguise.*]
Ex officio, my lords!

DE CHARTRES

Your secret shall be safe with us. — This, sirs,
Is Marshal Flavy.

LA TREMOUILLE
[*To Flavy.*]
From Compiègne?

FLAVY

I am

Commander at Compiègne.

LA TREMOUILLE
[*To De Chartres.*]
He knows the plan?

FLAVY

I am to ask the help immediate
Of Jeanne the Maid against the enemy
That threaten my city.

DE CHARTRES
I explained to him
How *this* good friend (*indicates Cauchon*) will see to
it that the English
Shall know the proper moment to attack
And lure the Maid to fight outside the walls.

FLAVY

A few French troopers will pass out with her,
And then — I am to pull the drawbridge up.

CAUCHON

She shall be treated by us justly, sirs,
By process of the law for heretics.

DE CHARTRES

She is coming : I will go.

LA TREMOUILLE

What! not afraid
To catch a second ague?

DE CHARTRES

In her presence
All policy deserts me, I grow blind;
Once was enough.

LA TREMOUILLE

Wait; we will go along
With you and fetch the King and Brother Richard.

[*Exeunt La Tremouille, De Chartres, Cauchon, and Flavy
(right).*

*Enter, at left (down scene), Jeanne. She is closely followed
by a group of various persons,— women, artisans, gentle-
folk, — some of whom, drawing near, touch her cloak,
try to kiss her hands.*]

SEVERAL VOICES

Holy! holy!   Hear us, Maid of God!

JEANNE

Good souls, what would ye ask of Jeanne the Maid?

A WOMAN
[*Holding out a swaddled bundle.*]

My babe is dead.   Her little body's cold.
Oh, resurrect her !

JEANNE
[*Tenderly.*]
Was thy child baptized?

THE WOMAN

Yes, Angelique.

JEANNE
Then do not cry for her,
For she is playing now at Mary's knee.

ANOTHER WOMAN

Mine's newly born.   Be godmother to him,
That he may prosper.

JEANNE
Let his name be *Charles*.

A COURTIER
[*Reaching out his palm.*]

My fortune, Maid !   When shall my luck change?

JEANNE

If

Your luck be lame, rub it with elbow-grease.

A KNIGHT

Jeanne d'Arc, my master sendeth me —

JEANNE

Who is

Your master?

THE KNIGHT

'Tis a nobleman of France,
And prays you tell him which of the two popes
Of Rome or Avignon he should obey.

JEANNE

Tell him with God there is no politics;
Let him serve God. — Why do you touch your rings
To mine, good people?

AN ARTISAN

To be sanctified.

JEANNE

Oh, do not touch my hands. But if ye seek
Blessing, go home and kiss the old tired hands
Of your good mothers that have toiled for you;
Come not to me; good night, friends, and adieu!

[*The people depart; Jeanne stands with hands clasped.
Enter from the tent Louis de Contes; seeing her thus,
he kneels before her, worshipful.*]

What shall I do? — Ah, Monseigneur in heaven,
Protect me from their prayers! Let not this folk
Commit idolatry because of me
Nor touch this body as a saintly thing.
Guard me, you dear and gracious Voices! — Still
Why do I think on what my duke he said:
" Do not believe them, Jeanne! They are delusions."

[*Shuddering.*]

Dear God, let me forget, for I am tired;
Let Thy work be fulfilled and take me home.

[*Seeing Louis on his knees, she drops impetuously beside him.*]
No, no! Not thou, my Louis!

LOUIS
                              Angelique,
Why do you weep?

[Enter D'Alençon through the cypresses behind them.]

JEANNE
                    The night — how great it is!
And we — how little and how weak we are!
That star is shining down on Domremy
Between the pear-tree boughs.   I had not dreamed
How that the world would be so great and wide.

LOUIS
They say it reacheth even beyond **Rome,**
Though I was never there.

JEANNE
                              It matters **not;**
It lieth all within Our Lady's arms. —
Tell me, my Louis, hast thou never **played**
At knucklebone?

LOUIS
            You will not play with **me!**

JEANNE
And may I not?

LOUIS
But you —

JEANNE
                        Sometimes **we play**
With pebbles; here are some.

LOUIS
                    But you!   From you

The English fled at Orleans, and to you
The angels speak and the bright saints come down!

JEANNE
[*Rising, drops the pebbles slowly from her hand.*]
It seemed but yesterday: in dear Lorraine
There was a lass with a red petticoat,
And she was called "Jeannette."

D'ALENÇON
[*Coming forward, impetuous.*]
                                    Madonna!
JEANNE
[*Starts, then goes to him.*]
                                              Thou!
            [*Turning back.*]
Ah, me! I saw it. Why did you stand there?

                    D'ALENÇON
Where, then?
                    JEANNE
                Behind you! Over my left shoulder
I saw it rising, pale.
                    D'ALENÇON
            [*Glancing off right.*]
                    The moon!

                    JEANNE
                                'Tis full.
What bad news have you brought me?

                    D'ALENÇON
                                    I?
                    JEANNE
                                The King!
What of the King?

D'ALENÇON
The King is well.

JEANNE

                                    But thou?
Thou art in pain, my duke.

D'ALENÇON
[*Looking at her.*]
                    It is not pain.

JEANNE
[*To Louis.*]
Go in and sleep.   When I have need of thee,
I'll call.

LOUIS
I will nap lightly, Angelique.
[*Exit into tent.*]

JEANNE
Now, now, my good knight, speak out plain: what
    news?
I cannot bear the sadness in your eyes.

D'ALENÇON
There is a sadness which belies its name
And grows immeasurably dear to joy.
The King —

JEANNE
        Ah!

D'ALENÇON
                He is coming here to-night
To speak with you.

JEANNE

　　　　　More counsels ?　In God's name,
Let us not hold so long and many parleys
But march short-cut to Rheims.

D'ALENÇON

　　　　　　　This town of Troyes
Holds for the English still.

JEANNE

　　　　　It will surrender.

D'ALENÇON

We have no engines for the siege.

JEANNE

　　　　　　I have sent
For Brother Richard.　He will open the gates
To-morrow ; the day after, we shall march
Straight on to Rheims.

D'ALENÇON

　　　　Charles will not march to Rheims

JEANNE

What shall prevent ?

D'ALENÇON

　　　　A vision from the Lord.

JEANNE

D'Alençon ! hath the King beheld a vision ?

D'ALENÇON

I did not say the King.

JEANNE

Who, then?

D'ALENÇON

A woman.

JEANNE

O bonny duke, why art thou strange with me?
Be not like all the rest, careful and slow.
Speak to me bold and plain.

D'ALENÇON

Forgive me, Jeanne,
My soul, too, is infected with this air
And breathes of weakness, innuendo, doubt;
But now, like thee, I will be bold and brief.
The woman Catherine de La Rochelle
Hath duped the Dauphin to believe in her
That she hath seen a vision out of heaven,
Declaring thee and all thy Voices false.

JEANNE

[*Scornfully.*]

Ha, by St. John! And doth she think to fool
My King with *fi, foh, fum?*

D'ALENÇON

The King believes.

JEANNE

[*Ardently.*]

Of course my King believes.

D'ALENÇON
[*Slowly.*]
In Catherine.

[*A pause: from off right come distant sounds of laughter, and a flickering glow.*]

THE VOICE OF CHARLES

Walk near us in the torch light.

D'ALENÇON
They are coming.

Madonna, do not let that scornful fire
Die from your face.   For such apostasy
There's a divine contempt which makes us strong
To suffer and retaliate.   Take heart!
What matters it though this half-minded prince
Goes begging for his crown. — Dost thou not hear me?

JEANNE

To build and build and build on running sands —
How terrible it must be to be God!

[*Reaching to D'Alençon her two hands.*]

Think you I shall be strong enough, my duke?

D'ALENÇON

Oh, I will give more than the world can take,
And fill the gap of this ingratitude
With burning recompense.   Lean thou henceforth
On me — on me —

THE VOICE OF CHARLES
[*Amid murmured conversation.*]
Enchantress!

JEANNE

'Tis my King.
Say I will welcome him within my tent —
And Catherine. This shall be overcome.

D'ALENÇON

But not alone! Let me stand with thee, Jeanne.

JEANNE

Always you are with me. When I close my eyes,
You lean against a pillar of the dark
And pore upon a book. You do not speak,
And yet I know whom you are reading of —
A certain queen — her name is hard to learn.

D'ALENÇON

Hippolyta!

JEANNE

A maiden-queen, you said.

D'ALENÇON

In Attica.

JEANNE

I know not where; good night!
Come not; this good fight will I make alone.

[*With a quick pressure of D'Alençon's hand, exit Jeanne
into her tent.*]

D'ALENÇON

"Always you are with me." — Did she say those
words,
Or am I dizzy with this incense of her?
" Say I will welcome him with Catherine."

What will she do? Well, I can but obey.
" Always you are with me!" Always, always ! Here—
On the air, this moonlight, everywhere — her face
Encounters mine in glory.

[*Enter Charles and* CATHERINE *attended by torch-bearers
and followed by La Tremouille,* BROTHER RICHARD, *and
Flavy.*]

CHARLES

[*To Catherine, holding her hand and gazing at her.*]
Even your shadow
Steals splendour from the moonlight — less a shadow
Than some bright spirit's reflection.

[*He kisses her fingers.*]

D'ALENÇON
God! Can that
Which leads him captive be akin to this
Which hallows me with beauty ?

CATHERINE
Charles is kind
To flatter his old comrade of Chinon.

CHARLES

Chinon! how our life-star hath changed since then !
Aye, Dagobert is dead, and poor King Patch
Is now a prince of Europe, thanks to — thanks
To God's aid and Saint Charlemagne, and now
Henceforth to you, sweet seeress. Tell me, Kate,
Of this white lady in the cloth-of-gold
That comes to you : when did you see her last ?

CATHERINE

To-night : her limbs were lovely as first snow,
And with her hand she touched me and said, " **Rise,**
And seek your King, and go forth in the land,
And let the royal trumpeters ride first
And blow nine blasts before you in each town,
And lo! all buried and concealèd gold
In France shall straight be gathered to your feet
In piles of glory. Give all to your King,
But tell him to beware the town of Rheims,
For if he enters there, my power is spent.

LA TREMOUILLE

Note that, your Majesty : the town of Rheims!
The vision warns you to turn back from Rheims.

CHARLES

We'll make this known to Jeanne and change our plans
Accordingly.
[*To D'Alençon.*]
She's here?

D'ALENÇON
There, in her tent,
And she hath bade me say —
[*Pauses.*]

CHARLES
What?
D'ALENÇON
[*Barely restraining his emotion.*]
Nothing, sire.
[*Exit swiftly (right).*]

K

CHARLES

[*Looking after D'Alençon in surprise, turns to Catherine and the others.*]

We will go in ; you also, gentlemen.

[*As he is about to enter the tent, the tapestry is opened from within by Jeanne, who stands in the entrance.*]

JEANNE

My Dauphin and the Lady Catherine
Are welcome.

CHARLES

[*Coldly.*]

'Tis some time, Maid, since we met,
And there are solemn matters to impart.
Come, Catherine.

[*Exit Charles into the tent.*]

CATHERINE

[*Aside to La Tremouille, as she follows Charles.*]

Why do you make me face her !

LA TREMOUILLE

[*Aside.*]

'Tis but a moment ; play the game well now.

[*Exit Catherine.   La Tremouille speaks to Jeanne.*]

This is Commander Flavy of Compiègne.

JEANNE

I pray you enter, sir.

LA TREMOUILLE

This, Brother Richard

Of Troyes.

[*Brother Richard, approaching slow, and suspicious, makes constantly the sign of the cross and scatters before him liquid from a vial.*]

JEANNE

What is he sprinkling?

LA TREMOUILLE

Holy water.

JEANNE

More boldly, sir; I shall not fly away.

BROTHER RICHARD

How know I yet whether thou art from God?

JEANNE

Enter and learn. — Come in, Sieur La Tremouille;
The room is small to hold both you and me,
But skilful driver turns in a sharp space.

LA TREMOUILLE
[*Pausing beside her.*]

'Tis you or I, Jeanne.

JEANNE

You or God, Seigneur.

[*They go in together, the tapestry closing behind them. Enter (right) D'Alençon and La Hire.*]

D'ALENÇON

'Tis shame enough, La Hire, immortal shame,
That she who hath for us her toil, her visions
Given in service, should be snared about
By webs of this arch-spider, La Tremouille,
To struggle and to suffer; yet 'tis worst
That he — that he, whom from a mockery

She hath made emperor, could so relapse
As to install this heinous substitute,
Rochelle.

LA HIRE
Not Catherine ?   Kate of Chinon !

D'ALENÇON
[*Bitterly.*]

She, too, hath visions — in Tremouille's brain —
Impugning those of Jeanne ; and Charles, her dupe,
Treats her with amorous credulity,
Half gallant and half gudgeon.

LA HIRE
                              This would make
The little flowers of Saint Francis swear.

D'ALENÇON
If they had but devised some common sham !
But to pry inward to her maiden soul
And steal that delicate and fairy stuff
The visionary fabric of a child,
Whose dreams of saint and seraphim take on
The sureness of reality — to make
Of that, I say, a tawdry counterfeit
To ordain the humbug of a courtesan —
No, it is monstrous !

LA HIRE
                Peste ! less metaphysic,
And say what's to be done.   Where is she ?

D'ALENÇON

There ;

The King and Catherine are with her.

LA HIRE

Well,

Trust her to make a charlatan turn feather.

D'ALENÇON

There is the pity of it! How may she,
Unconscious child, disprove in Catherine
The nature of illusions which her own
Imagination shares? — God spare her that!
For there's no pang, 'mongst all our mortal hurts,
Sharp as the vivisection of a dream.

LA HIRE

I love thee, friend D'Alençon, but thy mouth
Is stuffed too full of parchment. Pray, disgorge ;
What means all this ?

D'ALENÇON

No matter. (*Broodingly*) Once at Orleans
I spake harsh truth to her myself. God knows
I said it but to save her.

LA HIRE

By my stick,

What shall we do ? Go in there and smash pates ?

D'ALENÇON

That would be madness.

LA HIRE

What the devil, then ?

D'ALENÇON

This : I am strong in money and estates
And have a certain influence with Charles
Which I have never yet used : if he disowns
Jeanne d'Arc, then I will offer her my hand
In marriage.

LA HIRE

Thou ! thou — to the Maid of God !

D'ALENÇON

No, to the maid of Domremy — " Jeannette."
This is no time for superstitious cant ;
I must now serve her and be practical.
I am a duke and she is peasant-born ;
I, as her husband, would uphold her power ;
If she reject me — mine alone the pain.

LA HIRE

Dost thou not fear the wrath of God for this ?

D'ALENÇON

There is no God for me but human love,
Nor vision save the true vouch of mine eyes,
And human love and true vouch of mine eyes
Compel me to this act.

LA HIRE

How long hast thou
Run daft ?

D'ALENÇON

Jeanne ! Jeanne ! thou shalt not stand alone.

LA HIRE
[*To himself.*]

Fala ! This comes of poesie and parchment !

[*Hastening after D'Alençon, where he has gone toward Jeanne's pavilion.*]

Look ye, my duke, walk this way to my tent
And reassure me that thou be not mad.

D'ALENÇON

Indeed, for love of her, perhaps I am.

[*Exeunt at back, La Hire drawing D'Alençon away from the tent, from which — after a brief pause — Charles bursts forth, followed by Catherine and soon afterward by La Tremouille, who, standing at the entrance of the tent watching them, twists the tapestry with his fingers.*]

CATHERINE

Charles! Charles, my King! Forgive me.

CHARLES

                                    To forgive
Is simple: to obtain forgiveness — where
'Mongst all my fellow-men may I now look
To be forgiven.

CATHERINE

I am penitent.

CHARLES

Why, so am I; yet surely as that moon
Shall wane, so surely shall we lapse again.
Such creatures, Kate, as you and I are changelings,
Filched out of hell by Satan's forefinger
And smuggled into clouts of human kind
To mock at God the Father.

CATHERINE

                              Mine the sin;
I lied to you.

CHARLES

Hush! *I* lied to myself.
Who made me King of France? Whose vision smote
The clutch of England's armies from my throne? —

[*To his torch-bearers.*]

Go on! put out those lights, and if you can
Put out those stars! and thou, dear Maid of God,
Let me forget how basely I forgot.

[*Exit with torch-bearers. La Tremouille comes to Catherine,
where she stands trembling.*]

LA TREMOUILLE

Have we been drugged with wine?

[*Points to the tent.*]

What happened there?
I saw you speak to Jeanne, Jeanne look at you.
What was it she did?

CATHERINE

I know not what she did,
But what she *is* shone through her as a lamp
Into my wretched heart, and made me weep
To know myself. — Pray, lead me to my tent.

LA TREMOUILLE

Defeat once more; defeat! By Hercules!
For strategy to outwit the lords of Rome
Commend me to a sheep-girl from Lorraine!

[*Exit with Catherine. Within the tent is heard the voice of
Brother Richard.*]

BROTHER RICHARD

The city's gates shall open to the King.

[*Enter from the tent Louis, who holds aside the tapestry, staggering with sleepiness. As Brother Richard passes out, he pauses and looks back within; then turns, moved, to Louis.*]

Child, thou art hallowèd to be her page.

[*Exit toward the ramparts.*]

LOUIS

[*Drowsily.*]

I dreamt I was awake and marching — marching —

[*Sinking upon the near bench, he is overcome by slumber. Enter Jeanne and Flavy from the tent.*]

JEANNE

I promise you, Commander, I will aid
Your brave folk in their need. Bid them take heart!
As soon as I have crowned my King at Rheims,
I will go to help the good town of Compiègne.

FLAVY

Your coming shall be rarely welcomed, Maid.

[*Exit (right).*]

JEANNE

All will be over soon — my King be crowned!
Louis, come forth! We'll sleep under the sky;
The night is hot, it stifles there within —
Louis!

[*Discovering him.*]

Ah, weary boy! Thou art still marching

Toward Rheims. — Wait but a moment, little Louis,
Under our lids I'll overtake thee there.

[She lies down in her armour on the next bench and falls
asleep in the moonlight. Enter at back, D'Alençon and
La Hire. Seeing Jeanne, they pause, speaking together
in low tones.]

LA HIRE

Not if thy love were whiter and more chaste
Than Abelard's for his dead Heloise —
No, friend D'Alençon !

D'ALENÇON
               Will you answer me ?
A thousand common drudges, artisans,
Peasants and townsfolk daily flock to her
And kiss that hand in homage. — Am then I
Less worthy ?

LA HIRE
          They have faith in her.   They seek
Salvation.

D'ALENÇON
       For themselves !   I seek it for her.
This maid is holy by simplicity
And not by miracle.   She is a brave
And gentle girl, no more. — How noble she sleeps !
By Heaven, I will keep vigil here to-night.
I love her.   Do you trust my honour ? — Leave me.

LA HIRE
[Giving his hand.]
Good night, friend ; but beware the Lord His angels.
[Exit.]

D'ALENÇON

When did such maidenhood sleep in the moon
Before? Or such a soldier dream in armour?
The camp is silent and this summer night,
But all the dark is sown with dragon's teeth
That with the dawning shall spring up in steel
To rage and stab again. — What martial seed,
Dropt in the April lap of green Lorraine
By angels sacking hell from Sinai's mount,
Bourgeoned this armèd girl to captain us?
Here sleeps in silver the strong virgin — France.
She murmurs: What was that? — Dear God, my
    name!
"D'Alençon!" — Jeanne! Jeanne, leave thy dreams
    ajar
And let me through to thee — so, with a kiss.

*[As he springs to kiss her hand, he is caused to stagger back
    by a dazzling, intervening splendour, out of which there
    takes shape the winged form of St. Michael, holding his
    sword drawn.]*

Thou burnest me, beloved; I grow blind;
My brain is stung with fire. Where are thou snatched
In flame away from me? — Ah! — stand not there
Between us! Merely would I bend to touch
Her still hand with my lips and then begone,
And yet are you implacable? — Stern Saint,
Vision, or flaming Minister of Heaven,
Hallucination, or Apocalypse,
Whatso you are that, beautiful, take on
The likeness of imagination, why —
Why do you stand between us?

[*With his sword St. Michael strikes D'Alençon.*]

Monseigneur!

At last the knowledge and the sin of it,
The sinning and the beauty! — Lord, I go.
For thou art bridegroom to the Maid of God,
And she who lieth there is thy betrothed,
And I, that dared to love, have sinned.   Adieu,
Bright sentinel!   Thine is the vigil now,
The midnight and the Maid inviolate.

[*Exit D'Alençon among the cypresses.   A minute now passes
   before the curtain falls.   Various night sounds steal upon
   the scene ; distant torches flicker out ; and the murmurs
   and motions of a great army, camped, are suggested to the
   audience's imagination, while Jeanne — the virgin-cap-
   tain of that host — lies sleeping, moonlit, in her armour,
   guarded by the sentinel archangel, vigilant-eyed.*]

Scene II: A Street in Rheims.   July 17, 1429.

*The street itself is hidden behind an old, half-ruined wall of
   the city, over the irregular top of which are visible the
   upper windows, balconies, and gables of the houses oppo-
   site, from which the inmates are seen watching the
   crowds below, invisible to the audience.   The foreground
   of the scene consists partly of the wall itself, partly of
   an embankment (with a crooked, elevated foot-path,
   conducted by stone steps to different heights), which
   slopes upward to the wall's edge.   On the left, at a
   breach in the wall, is a wide ruined gate, admitting in-
   gress from the street on to the lower foreground left*

ACT FOURTH, SCENE II : A STREET IN RHEIMS

where the path starts to ascend the slope of the embank-
ment. Seated on the wall, or peering over it (where
they stand on the embankment foreground), and filling
the gateway, are varicoloured groups of persons.
Among these (right) are Pierre Cauchon and NICOLAS
LOISELEUR, *in the dress of artisans; near the gateway,*
amid a group of peasants, Jacques d'Arc, Perrin, Pierre
d'Arc, and Mengette. High in a seat of vantage on
the wall, a PRIEST *is looked up to by the people near*
by, as a presiding authority.

The following dialogue is spoken — with varying intervals
of pantomime — during partial lulls in the hubbub of
the hidden populace in the street, and the reflex of that
among the groups of the foreground.

As the curtain rises, there resound from the left a fanfare
and a vast, distant shout.

A CITIZEN

Those trumpets, father ?

THE PRIEST
[*On the wall.*]

Now the King receives
His crown in the cathedral, and the people
Acclaim the Maid of God.

PERRIN
[*To Pierre and Mengette.*]

Why were we late !
They say Jeannette stands next the King himself.

MENGETTE

And all in armour !

PIERRE

If she goes right by!
And if she never sees us!

JACQUES D'ARC

Fret thee not;
I ha' fetched from home a clinkle in my pouch
To catch thy sister's ear.

PIERRE AND MENGETTE

What is it?

JACQUES
[*Mysteriously.*]

Look!
[*Shows a string of little pewter sheep bells.*]

LOISELEUR
[*To Cauchon.*]

Your Reverence' disguise is masterly.

CAUCHON

Thanks, Nicolas; and yours!

A WOMAN
[*To Mengette.*]

From Domremy?
Aye, that's the town the King hath freed from tax
Because the Maid would ask no other boon.

MENGETTE
[*Anticipating her triumphant effect with blushes of pleasure.*]
I am her neighbour and her brother's wife!

CAUCHON
[*To Loiseleur.*]

Yes, much at stake! My kind friend Winchester
Hath promised me the archbishopric of Rouen —
When she is ashes.

LOISELEUR
That should not be long.
She goes hence to help Flavy at Compiègne.
At Compiègne there will be a witch for sale.

CAUCHON

Aye, Flavy knows the smell of English gold —
[*Looking from the wall.*]

How proud her pageant rides! The dust rolls up
Like smoke before her.

LOISELEUR
Soon it shall be *fire.*

CAUCHON

Look where she comes!

LOISELEUR
Who looketh where she goes?

[*The pageant has begun to enter. Above the wall are visible
the lances and halberds of the marching soldiers, their
standards and the floats of the pageant. From the left,
after the passing of several displays and devices, the
tumult and hosannahs roar and swell to a rhythmic,
pæan-like acclaim upon the entrance (as yet unseen by the
audience) of Charles and Jeanne.*]

THE PEOPLE

Noël! Noël! Noël! The Maid of God!

[*As this royal portion of the pageant passes beneath the central groups in the foreground, Jacques d'Arc at the gateway takes from his pouch the little pewter bells, and, raising, tinkles them in the uproar. As he does so, the throng in the breach itself are swayed inward and aside by a commotion from the street without, and Jeanne and the King appear in the gateway on horseback, their immediate followers — La Tremouille, De Chartres, D'Alençon, La Hire — being visible behind them.*]

JEANNE

[*Reining her horse.*]

My King!

CHARLES

[*Halting the procession, turns solicitously to Jeanne who, not yet seeing Jacques d'Arc and his bells, is listening with a bewildered look of pleasure.*]

What is it, Maid?

JEANNE

The sheep!

JACQUES D'ARC

[*Breaking from the crowd and going to her.*]

Jeannette!

JEANNE

Ah! — Papa Jacques!

PIERRE, MENGETTE, AND PERRIN

Jeannette! Jeannette!

JACQUES

[*At her horse's side.*]

My lass!

JEANNE

[*Kissing his hands where he raises them to her.*]

And art not angry with me?

JACQUES

God is good.

Thou hast served Him long, lass. Come now home
with me!

CHARLES

This is thy father?

JEANNE

May I go with him?

[*Showing the bells.*]

See, he hath fetched me these from home.

[*Waving her hand.*]

Mengette!

Perrin!—I did not knit the other mitten!

LA TREMOUILLE

Sire—

JEANNE

[*Turning quickly.*]

May I go? My vow to God is kept,
And nothing now prevents—

LA TREMOUILLE

Your promise, Maid.

Compiègne—

JEANNE

I had forgot!

L

LA TREMOUILLE
[*To the Procession.*]

Go on.

JEANNE
[*To the group with her father.*]

Adieu!

I must go to serve my good friends at Compiègne.

JACQUES

Thy mother!—waiteth for thee.

JEANNE
[*Tossing to Jacques the steel gauntlet from her right hand.*]

Show her this,
And tell her I would rather spin at home,
But for a web begun God sendeth thread
And I must spin for France.

[*The Procession begins to move; the crowd sways between Jeanne and her father, who stands, with bowed head, holding the gauntlet.*]

MENGETTE
[*Lifted from her feet by Pierre, tears off her head-dress and waves it above the people's heads.*]

Jeannette!

[*Jeanne, turning her horse and looking straight on, holds in her left hand her banner; in her right—close to her ear—the string of clinking bells, to the others inaudible through the cries of "Noël!" and the thunder of the cathedral chimes.*]

JEANNE

The sheep!

ACT V

ACT V

SCENE: Jeanne's Prison at Rouen. May 30,
1431.

*A dim room, with only one small, barred window (at back)
very high up. Doors, right (down stage) and left (up
stage). Massive stone pillars sustain the ceiling. Inconspicuous in the obscurity of the right upper corner
stands a narrow cage, with irons for the occupant's
neck and hands.*

*As the scene opens, a group of persons in black ecclesiastical
gowns is seen passing slowly across the prison chamber,
from the door of an inner room (right) to the outer
door (left). Among them are Pierre Cauchon and
Nicolas Loiseleur. They are followed by John Gris,*
BROTHER MARTIN LADVENU, *and the* CAPTAIN OF THE
ENGLISH GUARD. *In the background loiter* THREE
SOLDIERS OF THE GUARD, *coarse types of men-at-arms.*

CAUCHON

What think you, Nicolas?

LOISELEUR

                    Her spirit fails;
I fear she will not last.

CAUCHON

                    That will not do!
She cost too dear a penny at Compiègne
For us to let her now escape the fire
And pass like any Christian soul.

LOISELEUR

'Twere pity.

CAUCHON

And this long trial which hath lately closed
To end in farce! — Besides, the folk of Rouen,
That weep around this prison on their knees,
Will say we murdered her.   Whereas, i' the fire,
Not merely shall we brand her heretic
And witch, but we shall tarnish with her shame
The crown of Charles, which this said witch put on
    him.

LOISELEUR

Then, too, your Reverence' archbishopric
So nearly earned!

CAUCHON

Hush; nothing of that now.
We must make haste. — Captain, a word with you.

[*As Cauchon takes the Captain of the Guard aside, John
Gris speaks to Brother Martin.*]

GRIS

I was her prisoner at Orleans once,
And now her keeper! Would to God again
I were her prisoner, and she once more
In that proud freedom. — When did she begin
To doubt her Voices?

BROTHER MARTIN

After the great lapse,
When she recanted all in the open square,
Seeing the executioner's black cart

Awaiting her.   Since then, though she hath now
Resumed her man's garb which she then put off,
And docilely affirms her faith, yet she
Is shaken in her soul, for now no more
She sees her visions, hears no more her Voices.

GRIS

To what doth she ascribe this ?

BROTHER MARTIN

I know not.

A year of darkness and imprisonment,
And slow, sharp probings of the Inquisition
Have weighed on her bold spirit.   This I know :
That many an age your English hearts shall bleed
To hear the story which doth end this hour.

GRIS

[*Drawing closer to Brother Martin.*]

Where stays your Paris monk ?

BROTHER MARTIN

[*Secretively looking toward Cauchon.*]

The duke is still here ;
Three days I have concealed him in my cell,
But still have found no means to bring him to her.

GRIS

Means *must* be found.   I'll call the guard away.

CAUCHON

Thou, Brother Martin, come with us ; let stole
And Eucharist be brought for her last rites.

[*To the Captain.*]

You have your orders, sir.

[*To the Inquisitors.*]

Come, gentle masters,

This noon we'll lunch with long-earned appetites.

[*Exeunt (left) Cauchon, Loiseleur, Brother Martin, and the
    Doctors of the Inquisition. At the door, John Gris
    stops and speaks to the Captain of the Guard.*]

GRIS

The orders of my lord the Bishop you
Will execute with gentleness.   Remember
That you are Englishmen and she a maid.

[*Exit.*]

THE CAPTAIN

[*To the Guards.*]

Remember, too, my lads, how this same " Maid "
By damnèd arts hath sent ten thousand souls
Of Englishmen to hell.

FIRST GUARD

Comes now her turn.

THE CAPTAIN

Fetch here the prisoner and put on her
The garb of heresy.

[*Exeunt guards into the inner room, whence they return
    immediately, dragging Jeanne, one of whose feet is tied
    to a heavy log. From this they unchain her. She is
    dressed still as a man, in a worn, dull-coloured garb. In
    aspect she is very pale, and of a spiritual emaciation.
    From the cage in the corner, the Captain has brought a*

*long white tunic and a mitre-shaped cap, which he hands
to one of the guards, who prepares to put them upon
Jeanne.*]

JEANNE

Will it be now?

THE CAPTAIN

Aye, and forever after.

SECOND GUARD

There be piled
Kindlings in Rouen Square. After the Bishop
Hath spoke his sermon, there shall be a bonfire.

THIRD GUARD

They say the Square is packed.

FIRST GUARD

[*To Jeanne, lifting the tunic.*]

Come!

JEANNE

'Tis for me?

What are these, sir?

FIRST GUARD

The wedding cap and gown
That old Dame Inquisition gives her daughters
When they go to the Devil.

SECOND GUARD

He'll make her a brave

House-warming —

[*Saluting Jeanne derisively.*]

Hail to 's doxy!

THIRD GUARD

Hail her cap!

[*Taking it from her head, for Jeanne to see, he holds it aloft while the other guards, severally bowing and doffing before it, read the words which are blazoned on its surface.*]

THE GUARDS

Apostate! — Heretic! — Idolatress!

[*Reënter Brother Martin, with candles and stole. He stands in the doorway; behind him appears another cowled figure, which withdraws when the Captain speaks.*]

BROTHER MARTIN

I bring the last rites for the prisoner.

THE CAPTAIN

Whom hast thou with thee there?

BROTHER MARTIN

A monk from Paris.

[*Enter abruptly, in the doorway, John Gris.*]

GRIS

Captain, your guard is wanted in the court!

THE CAPTAIN

[*To the guards.*]

Come! — Jeanne, by order of my lord the Bishop,
Thou hast four minutes wherein to confess
And gear thy soul whither it goes. — Hear'st thou?

JEANNE

I hear thee, *godon.*

THE CAPTAIN

[*To Brother Martin.*]

The executioner
Is waiting in the court.   When you shall hear
His bell-cart tolling, come away.

[*Exeunt the Captain, John Gris, and the guards, the third
    guard handing the mitre-cap to Brother Martin, who
    sets it and the candles on the floor of the cell.   During
    the time in which the door remains open, sounds of dis-
    tant chanting come from without.*]

JEANNE

What voices
Are those?

BROTHER MARTIN

Priests chanting for thy soul. — My child,
I will return at once and bring thee comfort.

[*Exit (left).*]

JEANNE

They are not priests : that is the Judge's Clerk
Reading the questions in the Justice Hall ;
Day after day they lead me down to answer.
Do not you hear?   Those are the accusations,
And there are seventy.   He's crying them
Aloud in the open court.   He will not cease ;
And all the masters' gowns are turned to grey. —
Cease !   I have heard all, my lords !   Pray, bid him
    cease.

[*From behind the blank wall which Jeanne, clad in her
    white tunic, thus supplicates with outstretched arms,
    there rises, articulate, out of the far-heard chanting of
    the monks, and becomes loud enough for clearness — a
    monotonous, droning voice.*]

THE VOICE

And first, according to Divine Law, as according to Canon and Civil Law, it is to you the Bishop, as Judge Ordinary, and to you the Deputy, as Inquisitor of the Faith, that it appertaineth to drive away, destroy, and cut out from the roots in your Diocese, and in all the kingdom of France, heresies, witchcrafts, superstitions; to punish and amend all those who act against our Faith: to wit, sorcerers, diviners, invokers of demons, their abettors and accomplices. And your power as to this exists against all lay persons, whatever be their estate, sex, quality, and preëminence; in regard to all you are competent judges.

What have you to say to this Article?

JEANNE

Pass on!

[The Voice resumes with the same intoning monotony. Before it is done speaking, there softly reënters (left) Brother Martin, followed by D'Alençon. The latter is dressed in a robe and cowl similar to the monk's, but these are but thrown loosely over his usual garb. Jeanne neither hears nor sees them.]

THE VOICE OF THE CLERK

But it is time to instruct you more fully, my lords and judges, on the offences, excesses, crimes, and misdemeanours committed by the accused, Jeanne d'Arc, in many and diverse places. In her childhood she was not instructed in the beliefs and principles of our Faith; but by certain old women she was initiated in the science of witchcraft, divination, superstitious doings, and magical arts — so much so that, in these interrogations before you, touching her visions and the apparitions of fairies, she hath confessed that even now she doth not know if these fairies were evil spirits or not.

What have you to say to this Accusation?

JEANNE

I have answered you before. As for the fairies,
I know not what they are. But for my teaching
I was brought up to say my Creed, and do
Whatso a good child ought.

D'ALENÇON

Whom speaks she to?

BROTHER MARTIN

       Some phantom of her fever;
For pale hallucinations come to her,
No more her sacred visions; random voices —
The memories of her late torture-trial —
Not now her saints. Oft, as I told you, she
Will call your name.

D'ALENÇON

       Oh, that she call it now!

THE VOICE OF THE CLERK

Of Robert de Baudricourt Jeanne asked to have made for her a man's dress and armour appropriate. These garments and armour being furnished, Jeanne, rejecting and abandoning women's clothing, her hair cut around like a young coxcomb, took tunic, doublet, surcoat, close-cut cap, buskins, spurs, sword, lance, and other arms in fashion of a man, affirming that in this she was executing the order of God as had been prescribed to her by God's messenger.

[*Jeanne makes toward the wall a gesture of pathetic affirmation.*]

D'ALENÇON

Surely she hears some voice! — Is she so ill?

THE VOICE OF THE CLERK

What have you to say to this Accusation?

JEANNE

Pass on! It is so.

D'ALENÇON

Jeanne! *What* is so?

BROTHER MARTIN

She wanders.
Speak to her; but remember you yourself
Are under doom — an escaped prisoner;
Speak not too loud.

D'ALENÇON

Nay, let them find me. Death
Comes equitably now with her; and though
I am powerless to save her, yet 'tis sweet
Not to survive.

BROTHER MARTIN

Your will, then, is to be
Discovered and to perish?

D'ALENÇON

Here.

BROTHER MARTIN

If I
Consent, it is because *she* needs you : you,
Who first instilled her doubts, must extirpate them.
Farewell ; though she shall think you but a dream,
Yet speak ! — I will confess her — at the flames.

[*Exit.*]

D'ALENÇON

The flames ! — O Christ ! how dare I speak to her ?
[*Leaning faintly against one of the stone pillars, D'Alençon struggles for self-possession.*]

THE VOICE OF THE CLERK
[*Gradually sounding more remote.*]

Obstinate in her presumption, Jeanne hath said, proclaimed, and published that she recognized and discerned the voices of Archangels, Angels, and Saints ; and she hath affirmed that she knoweth how to distinguish their voices as of such ; she hath not feared to proclaim that St. Michael, Archangel of God, did himself come to her ; also that by revelation of Saints the crown of Charles the King was shown to him through her. All these are lies imagined by Jeanne at the instigation of the Devil, or suggested by demons in deceitful apparitions, to make sport of her curiosity — she who would search secrets beyond her capacity and condition.

What have you to say to this Accusation ?

JEANNE

What *should* I say, my lords ? — Yes, they were lies !

My Voices lied to me, my friendly visions,
That brought to me all holy signs of heaven,
They lied — they lied! for look, my masters: now —
Now I am brought before you in this hall,
And you command me to reveal you proofs
That what I saw was holy; now I call
On those bright saints to be my witnesses —
They come not, answer not! Ah, truly ye
Condemn me; I was tempted: demons were they,
And have deserted me, deluded me.

D'ALENÇON

Do not believe them, Jeanne!

JEANNE

You hear him, judges.
Even so he spake at Orleans, and I chid him.
My duke forewarned me well, yet I believed.

D'ALENÇON

Child, look on me. The latest moment, Jeanne,
Yet I am here : I too was prisoner,
Knew naught of this ; but when I heard, escaped,
And now I am come to witness to the truth.

JEANNE

My lords, you hear! Even he is come, a witness,
Before you.

D'ALENÇON

Not a witness before them, —
Your dread, grey judges, — but before those saints
And thy dear soul to attest their faith in you
And yours in them.

JEANNE

How pale thou art, my friend.
You must not sorrow now to speak against me.
You bade me doubt those visions, yet I kept
My faith ; the blame was mine. Well I remember
You warned me then they were but " vanities
And whisperings of the air."

D'ALENÇON

I knew not then —
JEANNE

How France should sell me to the English ! No !
Pass on ; 'tis over. — Will you address the court ?

D'ALENÇON

Here is no court nor trial-chamber, Jeanne.
Feel here — D'Alençon's hand ; this is your prison,
Where in a little moment Death shall enter
And lead us both away. I cannot bar
His coming, child, but I can make it happy
If this swift prayer can move your soul to hear.

JEANNE

To me you pray ? To me ? — They used to pray
To me at Rheims, and all the chimes were ringing.
[In the distance a harsh tolling resounds, and ceases.]
Hark ! they have begun again.

D'ALENÇON

That knelling bids
Me speak, nor hesitate. Jeanne, what I say
Is heaven and hell and life and death : I love you,
How — you shall know and understand. At first

I, now your anchorite, burned high for you
With man's desire.   Ere yet you came to France,
I caught afar the pastoral breath of you,
And sudden, when you'd come, you rose for me
Amidst our army's spears — a martial Ruth,
Bright from those rustled battle-sheaves of men,
And drew me, soul-bound. — 'I will love this child,'
I vowed, 'and win her love, for 'tis in sooth
A simple child, whose quick, religious heart
And pied imagination fill for her
The air with painted angels, speaking saints
And bell-toned voices.   Who that lives would not
Follow her eyes to Orleans and to Rheims?'
And so, a pagan in your holy war,
I followed you.   At last we camped by Troyes.
There in the moon, after the weary day,
While pale in armour you lay slumbering,
I kept my vigil.   Suddenly, your lips
Murmured "D'Alençon."   Ah! I leapt to kiss
Your sleeping hand — Jeanne! Jeanne! it rose
     between us
And smote me back!

> JEANNE
> My hand?
> D'ALENÇON

> > No, *his.*

> JEANNE

> > > What smote thee?

> D'ALENÇON

The mystery of you, the holiness,

For these — a blazing, keen, and two-edged sword —
That silent angel, radiant in wrath,
Did smite me with ; and lo ! with blinded eyes
I saw thee — what thou art : the Maid of God.
Angel, or saint, or guardian wraith — that blow
Made me to pray, to tremble, and believe.
I, who did boast to riddle a child's heart,
Was humbled and was glad.

[*The knelling resounds again.*]

JEANNE
[*Listening.*]
                                        Is it the cart?
I am afraid.   Art thou to go with me ?

D'ALENÇON
[*Gently.*]
Of course; and all your visions wait for you
To call them.   Child, let not my sceptic love
Lead your weak spirit to the world's dark sill
Thus stricken — blinded, groping for its saints
Believe! you who have made me to believe.

JEANNE
Why have they then forsook me — those sweet saints
That used to come — at least, methought they came.
Why do I not behold them any more?

D'ALENÇON
Because — remember what you told the King!
You must believe before you may behold !
But I — I wronged your faith.   Those noxious seeds
Of doubt I sowed in freedom — here, in darkness,

M

Prison, and pain, your black Inquisitors
Have fostered for their ends. *They* are your demons,
That have deluded you with sophistries ;
And if they ask for proof, say to them this :
Orleans is not a lie ; the gates of Troyes
Are not delusions ; no ! Rheims stands in stone ;
France — France is saved, and Charles the King is
    crowned !
Who hath done this but God and Jeanne, His Maid ?

JEANNE

Art thou a dream comest to tell me this ?
Or art my knight — my bonny duke ?

D'ALENÇON

Madonna !

JEANNE

It doth not matter ! — Though a thousand miles,
And clouds and towers and darkness are between us,
Still are you with me, absent, like a star.
Thou only knewest me, thou only knowest,
Save God, and thou hast brought me back to Him.
Look down, St. Michael ! Once again I wear
Thine armour : Lord, I dread no more the flames.
Lean down, St. Catherine, St. Margaret !
See, now I am your true girl — take my soul
And tell me you forgive, for I believe ;
Tell me you are true, and all my sin a dream !

[*Outside as the slow, harsh knelling resounds close by, high in
    the dim, barred window appear, in splendour, the faces
    (and, in part, the forms) of St. Michael, St. Catherine,
    and St. Margaret, who look down upon Jeanne.*]

THE FEMALE SAINTS
[*Simultaneous with the bell.*]
Thy pain — it is a dream.

JEANNE
[*With a cry of passionate joy.*]
My duke — they hear!
Behold they are come again! I see their faces,
I hear their voices!

D'ALENÇON
[*Kneeling beside her with bowed head, kissing the edge of her white robe, speaks to himself.*]
Would to God might I!

[*The door (left) is thrown open. In the passageway are heard heavy approaching footsteps and a murmur as of many people. Jeanne, standing, gazes up at the grated window — her face lit with a lost rapture.*]

THE VOICE OF BROTHER MARTIN
[*From outside.*]
The executioner.

ST. MICHAEL
[*His voice sounding with the approaching bell.*]
Be not afraid.

[*Away on the left, voices of men are heard chanting: " Kyrie eleison ! Christe eleison !"*]

FINIS

ADDENDA

In Act I, the refrain of the opening song is dialectical. In Act III, the letter dictated by Jeanne to the English is authentic; in the same act, the hymn, *Veni, Creator Spiritus*, known as the Hymn of Charlemagne, was historically sung by Jeanne and the French before battle. In Act V, the words spoken by the Voice of the Clerk are transcribed directly from the translation of the Seventy Articles, prepared by the Promoter d'Estivet, which formed the Accusation of Jeanne's Trial in Ordinary — published in the Appendix of the volume of Original Documents on Jeanne d' Arc, edited by T. Douglas Murray, New York, McClure, Phillips, & Co., 1902.

The author's sincere acknowledgments are due to Mrs. Patrick Campbell for her friendly interest in having specifically directed his attention to the above illuminating book, which has constituted the chief informing source, and a large inspiration, to his work.

The music of the play — incidental, as well as lyrical — has been composed by Mr. F. S. Converse, and may be had in published form.

The cover design and the scene illustrations of the present volume were drawn by Mr. Barry Faulkner.

The acting rights of the play, in America and England, are owned by Mr. E. H. Sothern and Miss Julia Marlowe.

PERCY MACKAYE.

CORNISH, N.H. September, 1906.